D0453768

Alex Leonovich:
A Heart for the Soul of Russia

San Diego Christian College
2100 Greenfield Drive
El Cajon, CA 92019

There is no doubt that God raises up special people to accomplish special tasks. Only God's sustaining Spirit in the life of Alex Leonovich can explain the selfless dedication that enabled him to burn himself out on the altar of service to his beloved motherland. As one who experienced some of the high excitement of his life with him, I thank Patricia Souder for capturing the fervor of this unusual man of God.

Dr. Joel Nederhood,
Former Speaker on "The Back to God Hour"

Jack and I have loved and admired Alex and Babs for many years now, so it is with great delight that we recommend this book which will take us to his roots and the reason God has so blessed [him]. . . . We learn valuable lessons from the lives and examples of the faithful.

Kay Arthur,
Precept Ministries

Alex Leonovich has devoted his life to the people of the former Commonwealth of Independent States whom he deeply loves. His passion for the work God has called him to has earned him deep respect from all who have had the privilege of working with him or sitting under his ministry.

Rick DeHaan
Radio Bible Class Ministries

In this life, I have two fathers. One gave me physical life and the second, spiritual. Alex Leonovich has been my faithful and wise spiritual father. . . . He, with his generous heart, loves Russia, America and above all else, God. I always thank the Lord for him.

Mikhail Morgulis, President
Christian Bridge and award-winning
Russian author and broadcaster

266.947
L/585A
S719a

ALEX LEONOVICH:
A Heart for the
Soul of Russia

One Man's Quest to Reach
His People for Christ

Patricia Souder

HORIZON BOOKS

A DIVISION OF CHRISTIAN PUBLICATIONS, INC.
CAMP HILL, PENNSYLVANIA

Horizon Books
3825 Hartzdale Drive, Camp Hill, PA 17011
www.cpi-horizon.com
www.christianpublications.com

Alex Leonovich: A Heart for the Soul of Russia
ISBN: 0-88965-174-4
© 1999 by Horizon Books
All rights reserved
Printed in the United States of America

01   02   03   04   05   6   5   4   3   2

Unless otherwise indicated,
Scripture taken from the
Holy Bible: King James Version.

Scripture references labeled "NIV"
are taken from the HOLY BIBLE:
NEW INTERNATIONAL VERSION ®.
© 1973, 1978, 1984 by the
International Bible Society.
Used by permission of
Zondervan Bible Publishers.

Scripture references labeled "NKJV"
are taken from the Holy Bible:
New King James Version
Copyright © 1982 by Thomas Nelson, Inc.

Contents

Foreword

A<small>LEX</small> L<small>EONOVICH</small> IS A direct, living answer to my prayers of many decades. I began praying for the people of Russia and the former Soviet Union in 1946. As a young businessman and a new Christian in Hollywood, California, I wrote my name on a large map of the world to pray for the people of Russia. I cannot explain this particular burden to pray in this way except that the Lord put it on my heart. I know it is because of God's great love for the Russian people. It is because of His compassion for them as they were under communist enslavement for seventy-two years.

Prior to communism, Russia had over 900 years of Christianity. It was rich in culture, literature, art, music and poetry, with vast resources of oil and precious metals. It was one of the great nations of the centuries. But then came the Russian Revolution in 1917 followed by seventy-two years of despotic, atheistic communism, when God was outlawed from every segment of society.

The great and wonderful people of Russia were victims of a cruel and godless system of tyrannical leaders who rejected the truth of God's Word, leading the nation totally astray, and murdering millions of their own citizens.

In 1917, the light went out in Russia. Or seemingly so. But the truth is, God left a light on. The great God of heaven was not without a witness. One of those witnesses was Alex Leonovich.

By God's great mercies, at about the same time I began praying for Russia, God was also using the prayers and evangelistic efforts of Alex Leonovich and his dear wife, Babs, to reach the Russian people with the powerful gospel of our Lord Jesus Christ. For many years, beginning in 1945, Alex's radio evangelistic efforts were a bright beacon of light in the darkest hours of Russian history. His radio ministry plus his visits to Europe and Russia, ministering to Russians in and out of their country, have been major factors in keeping hope alive in that great land. Only God knows how many souls he has encouraged and influenced in the kingdom through the years, but I know the numbers are great.

I have known Alex for many years, and am one of his greatest admirers. His life is an inspiration to me, and I know his story will be an inspiration to others. It is a great honor to know this great servant of God, and I thank and praise Him for Alex and his commitment and service to our wonderful Lord and Savior Jesus Christ, to whom be all the glory.

Dr. Bill Bright
Founder and President
Campus Crusade for Christ International

Introduction

Tanks crushing citizens in the streets of Budapest. Shoe-banging "We will bury you" speeches. Cutthroat power politics. The Cuban missile crisis. *Sputnik*. Nuclear warheads pointed toward Washington.

A succession of fear-inspiring specters threw a red pall over the Cold War world in which I grew up. I concluded that all Russians were communists bent on world domination and nuclear war.

A senior project on the Russian family jarred that perception. Love and longing, warmth and weariness, pain and pathos crept off the pages of a photojournalism feature I found in *LIFE* magazine. Perhaps Russians were real people unwillingly subjugated by a totalitarian regime!

Dostoyevsky and Tolstoy also challenged my simplistic views. Their masterful characters wrestled with good and evil, often highlighting the character and truth of God even in the midst of great suffering.

Years later, Alex and Babs Leonovich enfleshed the love and beauty of the Russian soul for me.

Our initial meeting was memorable, not because of Alex and Babs but because of my own provincialism. When told of Alex's Russian broadcasts, I thought, "How quaint. A nice little Russian program."

It was I who was little. Just because I hadn't heard "New Life" didn't mean it was small. Quite the contrary—millions of Slavs depended on Alex's shortwave program to beam truth and hope into their dreary, regimented world.

I didn't really figure that out until several years later when I started attending NRB (National Religious Broadcasters) conventions with my husband. There I heard Alex speak of his trips to the Soviet Union. Overflowing churches, an insatiable desire for God's Word, a confrontation with Madalyn Murray O'Hair at the Moscow Book Fair which was televised across the USSR—God seemed to be working overtime in the very land where officials had declared He didn't exist.

Alex's reports crackled with excitement, but I saw something else that fascinated me: a man of courage and conviction who simply did what he believed God was calling him to do. I was especially intrigued by his consistency in beaming short-wave gospel broadcasts into the Soviet Union for twenty years with only a few postcards and word-of-mouth comments to encourage him.

Wanting to know more about his inner workings, I began interviewing Alex in 1990. I discovered a man with an enormous heart and a story that needed to be written. His wife agreed wholeheartedly. Even Alex did not argue; he simply had no time to put it together.

I suggested a few qualified authors to God, but no one stepped forward. Meanwhile, a still, small voice kept troubling me.

That left me with an obedience issue. Although I felt inadequate for the job, I knew that Moses and Alex had felt the same way. Could I trust God to gift me to do what I believed He was calling me to do even as they had?

In 1995, my husband and I attended the RUEBU (Russian-Ukrainian Evangelical Baptist Union) Conference in Ashford, Connecticut, where we experienced robust bilingual services. With no understanding of any of the Slavic languages, we were definite misfits. Yet we, like the new immigrants, were warmly welcomed.

We met many people and learned many things. Mikhail Morgulis, President of Christian Bridge, and Ruth Shalanko Ertel, Peter Deyneka's daughter who is well known for her ministry to Russian women, expressed their enthusiasm for the project and eagerly contributed important chunks of information about Alex.

Later that summer, Alex and Babs invited me to spend several days with them, meeting and interviewing family, friends and staff. Their son, David, related lively tales from his growing-up years. Daughters Deena and Dawn told of their dad's willingness to stop whatever he was doing to get them a glass of water or bandage a scraped knee. Ken Lubansky, Deena's physician husband, and Dan Arthur, Dawn's husband, shared their perspectives while grandchildren bounded in and out of the dining room, obviously at ease in a family filled with love.

Lillian Ladisheff Lubansky told of Alex's leadership as a teenager. George Boltniew, Tim Semenchuk, Melody Ippolito, and Anne and Harry Lubansky helped me understand the work of Slavic Missionary Service and the breadth of Alex's ministry.

Nick and Rose Leonovich, Alex's brother and sister-in-law, told of Alex's boyhood and influence in their lives. Significantly, they have also invested their lives in reaching the Slavic people for Christ through a variety of ministries.

Doug Peters and David Pasechiuk of radio station HCJB and David Fisher and Bill Mial of TWR provided needed historical and technical details, as did Elizabeth and Constantine Lewshenia, Abe and Marge Van Der Puy and Ruth Moore Huntsberger.

Anita and Peter Deyneka of Peter Deyneka Russian Ministries and Dr. Mark Elliott of the Institute of East West Studies contributed valuable background material.

Jim Leonovich, Alex's nephew who is actively involved in Russian radio, described Alex's penchant for excellence and the effectiveness of his long-term ministry and current strategies.

Dr. Joel Nederhood, former speaker on "The Back to God Hour" and "Faith Twenty" championed the project while also providing great insights about Alex's ministry. He and Philip Yancey, author of *Praying with the KGB*, gave colorful accounts of their travels to the Soviet Union with Alex.

Dr. E. Brandt Gustavson, President of NRB, gave broadbrush perspectives. David Virkler, speaker on "The Word and the World" provided priceless tapes of interviews aired on his programs through the years.

Every source verified Alex's multifaceted ministry and full-fledged integrity. Nevertheless, I wanted firsthand witnesses who had been affected by his work. I dreamed of going to Russia to see the places where Alex had ministered but realized that my lack of funds and language skills made that impractical. Babs further warned that trying to go on one of Alex's trips would be impossibly exhausting because of his unstoppable pace.

Their daughter, Dawn, helped a great deal, for she had harbored a similar inquisitive spirit. Having grown up hearing the incredible stories her father told, Dawn decided to go see for herself the summer after she graduated from college. She was seated in the visitors' section of the church's balcony when church leaders invited people to write out prayer requests or greetings and send them to the front. Dawn thought this would be a good test so she wrote, "I bring you greetings from Alex Leonovich" and passed it forward.

When her note was read, the entire congregation gasped and turned around to see her. Dawn never doubted again.

God, however, always gracious, also honored my prayers for corroboration by sending several other special people my way.

The first was a quiet couple we met at a picnic at Wheaton College the weekend our daughter, Janelle, graduated. My husband, Larry, initiated a conversation with Mario and Larisa Vasic, parents of one of Janelle's suite mates. As he talked with them, he learned that Larisa had grown up in Belarus. Her father had been a pastor who was arrested several times, causing great deprivation for the family.

When asked if she'd ever heard of Alex Leonovich, Larisa became very animated, saying that her family had hidden under blankets every evening so they could listen to "New Life," a source of hope and truth during the dark days when they had no idea where her father was.

The next contact came through Inez Lear, a longtime family friend who told us about hearing Alexander "Sasha" Yuchkovski, a young Russian who had been persecuted for his faith while living in Moldova. She was so impressed with what he shared at her church's missionary conference that she sent me information about him.

I felt a little foolish calling someone I'd never met to ask if he had ever heard of Alex Leonovich. Sasha's enthusiastic answer exploded those fears as he credited "New Life" for much of his spiritual growth as a teenager. Currently, he serves as Chairman of the Executive Committee of SMS (Slavic Missionary Service), the organization Alex has headed for over forty years, an obvious evidence of the esteem Sasha holds for Alex and the work of SMS.

Thrilled with these serendipitous occasions arranged by God, I still longed for one more confirmation: the assurance that I understood some of the depth of the Russian soul. As I touched down at the Dallas-Fort Worth Airport to pick up the last leg of a flight home after a writers' conference in September, I whimpered a half-prayer for God to place a Russian next to me on the plane. When a tall young man with a small, strange-looking book in a foreign language sat down next to me, I caught my breath as I whispered, "Oh, God, this is so like You!"

And it was. Dmitriy had moved to the United States from the Ukraine seven years earlier. A graduate of a Russian medical school, he was on his way home from yet another disappointing interview in his quest to secure a place in a residency program. When I told him of my project and my prayer, he shrugged his shoulders and said, "Maybe God."

He followed that by the very question I was asking: "How can you write a book about a Russian if you're not Russian? You have to be Russian to understand what it means to be Russian."

I know Dmitriy is right, but I also know that God orchestrated our meeting to confirm His calling, for every bit of our conversation that day simply unveiled the Russian soul that Alex had taught me to see.

And the meeting wasn't just for my benefit. Dmitriy and I discussed politics, morality, social justice and faith with honesty and vigor. He told me of his Jewishness, his struggles with some of the stories of the Old Testament, his disappointments, hopes and dreams in life. I longed for Alex to be there so he could put his arm around Dmitriy and lead him to the One for whom his soul yearned.

I couldn't do that the same way Alex could have. But I did have something to give Dmitriy: the book in my lap, *The Jesus I Never Knew* by Philip Yancey.

Having read about thirty pages, I rifled through the pages from back to front to get a quick glimpse of what else was in the book. Only two names jumped out at me: Tolstoy and Dostoyevsky. Excitedly, I showed Dmitriy.

He shook his head sadly and said, "Too deep for me."

"No," I told him, "They're great Russian authors who talk about how to know God. You can understand them."

Later, I offered him the book. I knew what he would say before he said it: "But you haven't finished it."

I also knew the right answer: "I want you to have it. I can get another."

Alex had taught me well.

And God had shown Himself faithful.

I have done my best to verify the contents of this book. I recognize my limitations and accept responsibility for what I have written. I hope you'll enjoy the stories in this book and come to love and obey God better because of reading it. If you find mistakes, please let me know so corrections can be made in future editions or grant me mercy.

Regardless of your reaction, however, I am grateful for the privilege of working on this project. To Alex, Babs, their family, friends and coworkers, I say heartfelt thanks for opening your lives to me and beautifully demonstrating the goodness of God. To David Fessenden, my editor at Christian Publications, I say a big thank-you for believing in the book and seeing it through to completion. To my husband Larry, I say thank-you for helping to polish the final manuscripts and for your patience, encouragement and love throughout the project.

To the God and Father of us all, I bow in humble gratitude, delighted to once again acknowledge the truth of what William Cowper wrote in 1774,

"God moves in a mysterious way, His wonders to perform.. . ."

To God alone be glory,

Patti Souder
November 4, 1998

Believe to the end, even if all men went astray and you were left the only one faithful; bring your offering even then and praise God in your loneliness.

—Father Zossima in
Feodor Dostoyevsky's
The Brothers Karamazov, 1880

CHAPTER 1

ONE HUNDRED EYES
1965: Leningrad, Russia.

"REFUSED."

Alex Leonovich had seen the same word of rejection stamped on every request for a visa to visit the Soviet Union from the time he started submitting applications at the end of World War II until October 1965.

Now, after waiting for two decades, he and Dr. Ivan Kmeta, President of the Russian-Ukrainian Evangelical Baptist Union (RUEBU), stood in line to clear customs at the Leningrad International Airport. Alex's pulse quickened as he listened to the officials' cold, clipped tones and watched their stern, piercing eyes. The atmosphere crackled with tension.

What will they do when they come to me? he wondered, fully aware that Soviet officials were reinstituting many

11

of Stalin's hard-line policies that had been softened when Nikita Khrushchev had moved to de-Stalinize the USSR in the late 1950s and early 1960s.

Alex's excitement at finally being allowed to visit the land of his birth was tempered with warnings he'd received from the Russian church leaders who had attended the RUEBU Convention in Ashford, Connecticut, earlier that summer.

"Be careful, Alexei Pavlovich," they'd told him as they discussed the possibility of his visiting his native land. "One hundred eyes will watch your every step. People are suspicious of you because the government calls you a traitor who is using religion as a tool to promote capitalism."

Traitor—the very word conjured up horror and terror. Horror because Alex loved the land of his birth and carefully avoided promoting a political agenda over his radio broadcast. Terror because truth carried little weight when someone was targeted for persecution at the hands of the communists.

Alex wondered how widely such charges had circulated. He'd learned about them in 1964 when a friend, Pavel Boyko, sent him a copy of *Trud* (*Work*), a Russian newspaper purchased at a *kiosk* in Warsaw, Poland. In it, Alex had been called "an enemy of the state and a traitor to the Motherland" because of his shortwave radio program entitled "New Life."

How had Pavel managed to pick up that particular newspaper on that particular day? Had there been similar stories in other publications? Were they still being circulated?

The allegations frightened Alex but also projected hope. Perhaps people really were listening to his program! Otherwise, why would *Trud* denounce him?

Alex had been broadcasting for twenty years, encouraged only by scattered word-of-mouth comments and a few postcards which had escaped Soviet censors or been sent from neighboring countries. There were never good answers for the scores of people who asked, "How do you know anyone is listening? Only a few have radios. Besides the communists jam radio signals from the West."

Alex knew it seemed foolish, but he loved the Russian people and believed God had called him to broadcast the gospel to them, so he continued. He longed to know whether they were listening.

Realistically, though, how much would he learn in this strictly controlled society? And as a husband and father, was the risk he was about to take justified?

Although a naturalized American citizen, Alex was still considered a citizen of the Soviet Union because he was born in Belarus. Far from being a badge of protection, however, his dual citizenship meant he could be stopped at any time, for any reason. If arrested, he could be sent to prison, a mental institution or a labor camp in Siberia where, like his uncle, he could die as a martyr for his faith.

Alex's heart skipped erratically and perspiration drenched his palms as he came to the front of the line.

He hoped he'd get a male customs officer because friends had warned him that the women agents took their responsibility more seriously, attempting to outdo their male counterparts with their irksome fastidiousness. To make matters worse, the female agent at this customs counter wore such a stern facial expression that those in line avoided looking at her as they shifted their weight nervously.

Unfortunately, when she barked, "*Slehdueyouschy!*" ("Next!"), it was Alex's turn.

Attempting to defuse the tension, Alex smiled at the grim-faced woman and said, "It's wonderful, after so many years, to stand on the soil of my birth."

Ignoring his remarks, she commanded, "*Otkroitye chemodan!*" ("Open the suitcase!")

Alex swallowed hard as he unlatched the suitcase. He feared that what she was about to see would create an outburst, because, determined not to smuggle, he had packed six leather-bound Russian Bibles and a few pieces of Christian literature right on top of his clothes.

"*A eto shtaw?*" ("And what is this?"), she asked sharply.

Forcing a smile back to his face, Alex replied, "*Eto Bibleeyee.*" ("These are Bibles.")

"This is strictly forbidden here," she told him.

With his heart hammering so loud he was sure she would hear it, Alex showed her his visa and explained, "We are official guests of the Russian Baptist churches. You can see that our visas were granted by the Soviet Department of Religion and Cults. You know that in our culture no one comes to visit with empty hands. As official guests, we want to leave at least one Bible and some other piece of literature in the churches we are permitted to visit."

"Wait here while I speak to my superior officer," she told Alex as she took his visa and disappeared behind imposing doors.

Anxiety reigned until she finally returned and said brusquely, "Here's your visa. Keep this with you at all times."

Alex had no idea what had transpired in the officer's quarters, but he was grateful to have cleared the first hurdle in the unknown marathon that stretched before him.

A small group of Christians greeted Dr. Kmeta and Alex as they passed through customs. One of them whispered, "They're already here watching you."

Alex felt a chill go through him as he realized that every move and gesture he made could, and probably would, be scrutinized. Worse yet, since all the people around him were strangers, he had no idea if they were fellow travelers or KGB agents.

A sense of responsibility weighed heavily on Alex: how he and Dr. Kmeta conducted themselves would have rippling ramifications not only for them but also for the churches throughout the USSR.

In an unprecedented thaw in the Cold War, a delegation of four Russian pastors had been allowed to attend the RUEBU Conference in Connecticut in August. The current visit had been approved as a reciprocal one with Dr. Kmeta and Alex becoming the first evangelicals to be invited as official guests of the All-Union Council of Evangelical Christians-Baptists (AUCECB), an historic event designed to show the outside world that the Soviet Union had religious freedom.

The Russian Christians were allowed to give Alex and Dr. Kmeta only a brief welcome before the Americans were directed to the Soviet Intourist Agency where they were required to register. Known for being the arm of the KGB which monitored visitors, Intourist coordinated and controlled all travel arrangements within the Soviet Union.

Polite but firm, the Intourist agent demanded that he see everything in the Americans' pockets. Trained to intimidate, he fired questions at Dr. Kmeta and Alex while seeming to look right through them. After examining everything thoroughly and verifying their letters of invitation, visas, passports and itineraries, he asked, "Are you bringing any Christian literature with you?"

Alex again explained that Russian etiquette required them to bring gifts.

The agent accepted the answer and motioned Alex and Dr. Kmeta to a medium-sized black Volga driven by an Intourist chauffeur.

As they began their trip to their assigned hotel, the visitors sensed they were being micro-monitored. No amount of surveillance, however, could keep them from observing Leningrad's culture and history.

Known as St. Petersburg for 200 years, the city had been designed and built by Peter the Great in the early eighteenth century as a showcase of European architecture. When the communists took over, they renamed the city Leningrad.

Despite the government's attempts to obliterate the past, Alex felt prickles of excitement shoot through him as he looked at the massive monuments and numerous statues they were passing. Though silent, they still spoke of a great people and a great heritage.

Yet an oppressive pall seemed to suffocate the city. Although impressive, Leningrad seemed shrouded with a haunting, colorless, worn-out beauty. Its people dressed in drab grays and blacks to match their somber expressions. Coverall-clad women dug ditches with shovels and swept streets with thin willow brooms. They did their work thoroughly: No leaves lay in the street even though it was early autumn.

The very absence of leaves accented an artificial, forced listlessness that whispered despair. As Alex watched the city stream past the windows of the Intourist taxi, he grieved over the centuries of suffering his people had endured. Stalin's purges and repeated military operations had cut down millions of those who shared Alex's Slavic heritage. Women were compelled to do heavy labor because their husbands and sons had been killed. Nearly every family knew firsthand the wrenching pain of injustice and persecution.

It's as if the people have lost their will to live, Alex thought as he watched people performing tasks with all the grace of mechanical windup toys.

As they approached the hotel, Alex noticed that its large columns reflected the craftsmanship and charm of an earlier age. Uniformed doormen stood guard at the entrance, demanding proof of reservation before allowing anyone to enter.

Once inside the hotel, Alex spotted a man sitting in the lobby pretending to read a newspaper. The man's eyes peered above the paper, following their every move. Nearby, a woman spoke into a portable radio. Snatches of the conversation indicated she was reporting their arrival to her superiors.

Hotel staff checked their identity, assigned them room numbers and escorted Alex and Dr. Kmeta to their rooms. A floor monitor radioed their arrival. No one smiled and although they used the casual, familiar form of names when addressing each other, they did so in harsh, cutting tones.

That evening Alex telephoned Pastor Kjerukhansev of the Leningrad Baptist Church to let him know of their safe arrival and to make arrangements for the following day. The pastor said he would take them to a restaurant for breakfast at 8 a.m.

The next morning, the desk clerk announced, "I understand that you will be leaving at 8 a.m."

Alex knew immediately that someone had monitored his telephone conversation and made a mental note: The 100 eyes are linked to 100 ears!

While eating breakfast, Pastor Kjerukhansev warned the two visitors of concealed microphones in their hotel room. "Don't speak unless you have the volume on your radio turned high," he told them.

"The only safe places to converse are while walking outside or eating in restaurants. We're not allowed to entertain foreign guests in our homes and KGB agents will be present in the church services."

"Since you have been traveling around the clock," the pastor added, "we'll go to the evening service rather than the morning one today."

◊ ◊ ◊ ◊ ◊ ◊ ◊

That afternoon, Pastor Kjerukhansev met Alex and Dr. Kmeta at the hotel so they could ride to the church together. Knowing the Intourist chauffeur was monitoring what they said, they chose their words carefully.

As they neared the Leningrad Baptist Church, Alex saw masses of people huddled together under umbrellas because it was snowing. Since the service was not scheduled to begin for three hours, Alex asked, "What are these people doing?"

"They're here for the service," Pastor Kjerukhansev told him.

Amazed, Alex asked, "With all of these people here already, why don't we start the service now?"

Pastor Kjerukhansev shook his head quietly and answered, "Brother Alex, we can't, because if we did, they'd simply be here even earlier next time. Soon there'd be no semblance of order at all."

To avoid the crowds, Pastor Kjerukhansev took Alex and Dr. Kmeta into the church through a rear entrance in a lower room. Again, Alex couldn't believe his eyes: Forty elders were on their knees praying for the service.

"Is this a special day?" Alex asked.

"No. Our elders spend every Sunday fasting and praying so the Holy Spirit will work. Although we aren't allowed to give an invitation in the service, we pray that the Lord will touch hearts and people will come to God," the pastor explained.

When the pastor introduced Alex and Dr. Kmeta to the group, the elders gasped with recognition. Then they invited the visitors to join in fervent prayer until time to start the meeting.

When they finally walked onto the platform at 6 p.m., Alex thought his heart would stop: 1,800 people peered up at him in a building designed to hold 450!

The crowd was so dense that all chairs had been removed and all windows opened to deflect the corporate body heat. Yet despite cramped conditions, the people stood shoulder to shoulder with uplifted, expectant faces.

How incredible that people would wait so many hours in such uncomfortable circumstances! Alex thought, re-

membering there were also hundreds of other worshipers standing outside in the snow. *All of this when
everyone knows that there are KGB agents here whose
reports can result in harassment or arrest!*

Alex felt a giant lump fill his throat as Pastor
Kjerukhansev opened the service with the greeting,
"Peace be to you, dear brothers and sisters."

The congregation thundered back, "With peace we
receive you."

Then they sang heartily:

> How blest I am that Jesus Christ is my
>   Savior,
> That He is preparing a place for me in
>   heaven above.

Alex remembered the hymn from his boyhood and
wanted to sing along. Instead, he began to weep.

"All I could think of was how much these people
had been oppressed and hurt," he recalled. "They'd
been denied opportunities for education, work and
housing; they had lost loved ones in wars and purges,
yet they were singing about how fortunate they were. I
was deeply moved by their fervor and faith."

When the pastor introduced Alex, an audible gasp
erupted from the congregation. "What does that
mean?" Alex asked.

An associate pastor answered, "It means that everyone recognizes your name because they listen to your
radio broadcasts."

Alex felt a wave of gratitude well up within him. His decades of preparing and producing radio broadcasts had not been wasted! People had been listening even though the government insisted that there was no God and openly persecuted Christians!

Tears flowed freely and excitement mounted as Alex spoke.

When the service ended three hours later, a wall of people surged forward to touch him, shake his hand, hug him or kiss him Russian-style on both cheeks and then the mouth. Hundreds of people pressed in upon him to tell him that his radio broadcast was their lifeline, their means of spiritual nourishment, their way of experiencing fellowship with Christians from other lands and a primary source for teaching their children under an atheistic, totalitarian government.

Alex couldn't believe what he was hearing. "I had no idea so many people were listening, because they were not allowed to send mail to the United States. I was so glad that I hadn't given up when times were tough. And I was absolutely overwhelmed that God would allow me to see such fruits for my labor."

Who is this extraordinary man who persevered in doing what he believed God had called him to do when others called it foolish? What are his roots—and the secrets of his success?

When Christ came into my life, I came about like a
well-handled ship.

—Robert Louis Stevenson

CHAPTER 2

SOPLI SAILOR BOY
1922-1929: Sopli, Belarus

FIVE-YEAR-OLD ALEX studied the older boys as they
swished their nets through the canal water. His blue eyes
sparkled as he watched them dump one wriggling fish after another into their boats. He loved the way the fish
shimmered in the sun. *I'd like to do that*, he thought.

Alex glanced at his mother, but she was busy visiting with the other women of Sopli. *Maybe it would be
better not to bother her anyway*, he decided as he scam-
pered down the bank and pushed an old wooden rowboat into the canal.

Alex jumped in just as the boat began to leave the
shore. He teetered a little as he stood in the center of
the boat. It felt a little unsteady and scary, but overall,
he liked the sensation of drifting down the canal.
"This is fun!" he said as he watched the shore move
away from him.

The boat was just beginning to move a little faster when he heard his mother's voice: "Alex! Alex, come back. I have something for you."

Her voice was quiet, but insistent. Alex knew she meant business. Besides, she said she had something for him and he liked surprises.

But how can I get back? Alex asked himself, noticing that he was surrounded by water.

"Alex, sit down," his mother called.

Alex sat.

"Now put the oars in the water and pull."

Alex struggled with the oars. They were heavy and clumsy and he had a hard time getting them into the water.

"Pull, Alex, pull!" his mother shouted.

Alex tugged on the oars as hard as he could. The boat slowed.

"Good boy! Now lift the oars out of the water and do it over again."

Eager for the promised reward, Alex tried to do exactly what his mother told him. When he finally got the boat close to shore, his mother grabbed the boat and pulled it up on land. Then she gave Alex the surprise of his life: a memorable encounter with a young birch branch.

The switching stunned Alex. He cried bitter tears as the supple switch stung his bottom. This certainly was not the kind of surprise he'd hoped for! *How could something that was so much fun be so wrong?* he wondered.

Alex felt cheated and confused. Rebellion rose within him, but before he could give vent to his anger, he heard his mother start to cry. In a broken voice she said, "It hurts me to do this, but I must teach you to never do such a thing again. You could have been killed."

Killed? The thought hadn't even crossed Alex's mind. *Was what I did really that dangerous?* he asked himself.

His mother's tough stance coupled with her tender tears convinced Alex not only of the danger but also of her concern for him. Alex swallowed his indignation and sobbed, "I'm sorry."

As he did so, his mother enveloped him in a warm hug.

◊ ◊ ◊ ◊ ◊ ◊ ◊

For young Alex, the lessons of growing up revolved around his mother, Natalie. Theirs was a closeness forged by the hot flames of necessity and adversity.

The little sailor who launched the rowboat that day demonstrated his innate curiosity and love for adventure. His mother tempered his bravado by teaching him obedience and respect . . . essential ingredients for acquiring the resilience he would need to stay afloat in life's unknown, turbulent and ever-changing currents.

On the surface, life in the little village of Sopli, Belarus challenged the very notion of change. Each family kept a cow and a few chickens, ducks or pigs. They planted and harvested wheat, cabbage, potatoes

25

and turnips by hand. They made bread by grinding the wheat into flour with a grindstone. They drew water from the village well.

In the summer, wildflowers grew from their thatched roofs. In the winter, snow buried their cottages. Day followed night and spring followed winter as life plodded on in almost the same way as when the Slavs settled this land of swampy marshes and dense forests around 200-500 A.D.

Good workers but poor leaders, the Slavs had been dominated by stronger people groups, such as the Khazars, Vikings and Tartars, until 1480 when Ivan the Great united several rival principalities to overthrow Tartar rule and become the first Russian czar.

In 1905, Russia and Japan went to war over Manchuria. Russia lost. The tensions surrounding that war, losses to the Germans during World War I and Rasputin's evil influence over a weak czar eroded Russian morale. This paved the way for a revolutionary group of Russian Marxists known as the Bolsheviks to force Czar Nicholas II from his throne on March 12, 1917, ending 437 years of czarist rule.

In the months that followed, the Bolsheviks staged a campaign of sabotage and violence known as "the Red Terrors" before seizing the Winter Palace and arresting members of the provisional government on November 7. This takeover led to a massive civil war as the Bolsheviks, later known as communists, attempted to consolidate their power.

In an attempt to preserve Belarus' independence, anticommunists established the Belarussian Democratic Republic on March 25, 1918. It lasted only until January 1, 1919, when the Red Army took control and renamed it the Byelorussian Soviet Socialist Republic. Poland controlled some of Belarus until 1939, but most of it was incorporated into the Union of Soviet Socialist Republics (USSR) in 1922.

As the civil war raged, industrial production fell to one-seventh of prewar levels and farm productivity to one-half. In 1921 and 1922, a severe drought compounded the problems by wiping out most of Russia's grain crop in certain areas. Nearly 7 million Russians died of starvation in a two-year period, despite relief efforts by the United States.

The Leonovich clan feared they, like so many others, would starve. In desperation, they pooled their money to send someone to America in search of better conditions. Alex's father, Paul, was chosen as their representative.

Paul left Sopli in the spring of 1922. He found backbreaking work in the coal mines of Pottsville, Pennsylvania, and immediately began sending packages of food and clothing back to his relatives in Sopli. His first son, Alexei Pavlovich, "son of Paul," was born four months later on August 10.

Alex entered the world dramatically, weighing thirteen pounds. By contrast, his mother was a tiny woman, standing only four feet, eleven inches tall.

As she gazed at the little boy in her arms, she saw pale blue eyes; plump, dimpled cheeks and a thick mass of dark hair so typical of their long line of Slavic ancestors.

She also saw a challenging future, for she had a new baby to care for while her husband struggled to provide for them an ocean away.

Whatever her thoughts, however, Natalie Leonovich refused to waste time wishing things were different. Instead, the day after Alex was born, she pulled on her black work boots, donned her long homespun linen skirt and apron, tied her kerchief tightly under her chin and carried Alex to the community fields where she rejoined the other villagers as they harvested wheat with their hand sickles.

Astounded at Alex's size, the women joked, "He's so big, he'll have to start school soon!"

Alex learned to coo as the women harvested wheat, vegetables and sunflowers. When the days grew cold, he was placed in a sheepskin and laced to his mother's back so she could help store vegetables in the large hole lined with hay for insulating their precious food supply from subzero temperatures.

Winter brought fierce winds and snow so deep that Natalie had to dig tunnels through the drifts to feed the chickens, pigs and cow which were kept in a shed near the house.

She and Alex hovered near the large cookstove which served as their only source of heat. When the fire died out, she placed Alex's basket on the rear of the stove where grain and beans were spread out to dry. Then she talked and sang to him as she did her household chores and spun flax into linen on her spinning wheel.

As soon as spring warmed the air, the villagers returned to the fields to plant their seeds. Enchanted by the folk songs the women sang as they worked, Alex eagerly added his infant voice to theirs, learning to sing before he could talk. As the birch trees rustled and bowed overhead, Alex played in the dark, loamy soil, oblivious to political-economic problems and the difficulties his family faced.

◊ ◊ ◊ ◊ ◊ ◊ ◊

Although Natalie faced daily challenges to provide for her growing son in a land where so many were starving, another question constantly troubled her: How could she please God?

A devout woman, Natalie had always attended church faithfully. She learned a lot about God from the priests and always tried to do what they said. No matter what she did, however, God still seemed distant and she felt empty.

One day in 1924, two lay evangelists visited Sopli. "Jesus came to die for your sins so you can know God personally," they told the villagers.

Natalie listened carefully as the men explained how to become a child of God by believing in Jesus. As soon as she understood, she responded eagerly.

Excitedly, she wrote to her husband saying, "I've found what I've been searching for. How wonderful if you too would come to know God and receive Him into your life."

Incredibly, at almost the same time, Alex's father visited some Russian friends who lived in Passaic, New Jersey. When he walked into their home, he saw an open Bible on their table instead of the usual bottle of vodka. When it was time to eat, they invited him to join them as they prayed.

Paul wrote to his wife, "They prayed so earnestly and with such faith that it made me feel as if God was standing right there in the room. It was so real I opened my eyes and looked around, expecting to see God.

"I couldn't see Him, but I went with my friends when they invited me to a gospel service in a Russian church. I never saw such happy faces or heard people sing so beautifully as they did at that service.

"Then they stood up and spoke about their faith . . . I realized that I needed for myself what they had and I invited God to come into my life. How wonderful it would be if you too would give your life to God so that we could bring up our family in the knowledge of God."

Their letters crossed on the Atlantic! Within days of each other, Alex's mother in Belarus and his father in far-off America had each come into a personal relationship with the living God.

Eager to grow in their faith, both parents began meeting with other new believers.

For Alex and his mother, that meant an eight-kilometer walk each Sunday (about five-and-a half miles) to Gorodyets, the nearest village with a meeting place for believers.

Natalie's newfound faith puzzled the other villagers. Why would she want to go to a strange church in another village, especially when she had to take a toddler as big as Alex with her? And why wouldn't she dance and drink with them at the village revelries? In disgust, they shook their heads, kept their distance and called her *"Shtundistka"* ("Praying Baptist").

Natalie found her new faith and church family so vital, however, that she refused to let their ridicule, the difficulties of toting a toddler so far or bad weather keep her from a service. Unless she was sick, she made the journey. She was delighted when her brother, Daniel, joined her and became a believer.

Church and Scripture memorization became important priorities for Natalie and, in turn, for Alex. This led to Alex's first attempt at preaching.

Having listened to many adults share Scripture and what it meant to them in the church, three-year-old Alex decided to do the same thing.

He started by quoting John 3:16, the first verse he'd learned. Then he thought, *If they preach, I'm going to preach too.*

Alex launched into a detailed description of how the family had gotten ready for church that morning. He finished by saying, "When my uncle came, he got his coat and put his hand in the sleeve. Out jumped a mouse and everybody screamed."

The congregation erupted in laughter.

Alex felt confused. *Nobody laughs when the older people preach. Why should they laugh when I do?* he wondered.

Alex's mother could feel his bewilderment and put her arm around him as he sat down. Then, biting her lip to keep from laughing, she said, *"Vsjo khoroshaw"* ("Everything is OK").

Embarrassed, Alex stopped "preaching" at church. His inclinations in that direction didn't stop, however; they simply found new outlets.

Once Alex found a mole that had died. Feeling sorry for it, he carried the mole to a special place in the backyard where he carefully dug a hole to bury it. Then he sang "Oh, Happy Day," pounded a cross in the ground and preached a funeral sermon.

As Alex grew, he learned the Russian alphabet as well as Bible verses. Letters fascinated him and he started asking to see where the verses were in his mother's Bible. While looking at the words, he began to notice that certain words always contained the same letters. Before long, he began to teach himself to read.

Because his father was gone, Alex spent a lot of his time at his Uncle Daniel's. There, Alex's days were filled with the smell and feel of fresh wood shavings while he learned the basics of simple carpentry by watching his uncle make cabinets, tables and chairs. Daniel treated him kindly and Alex grew to love his uncle and to think of him as a father.

When Paul Leonovich came home in 1927, Alex refused to have anything to do with him. To Alex, the tall, lean stranger was an intruder who was cutting in on Alex's exclusive relationship with his mother, trying to replace the man who had acted as a father to him, and, in general, upsetting Alex's stable little world.

Paul understood his son's reluctance. A soft-spoken, perceptive man, he was hurt by Alex's reaction but responded by surrounding his son with quiet affection. Whenever he could, Paul explained gently that he had gone to America to work so life would be easier for Alex and his mother. It took many months, but Paul's patient kindness finally softened the little boy's heart and Alex gradually began to love his father.

It wasn't long, however, before there was another "stranger" in the Leonovich household to contend with. On October 1, 1928, Alex once again found his close relationship with his mother disrupted when his brother, Nicholas, was born.

As the family adjusted to many changes and challenges, economic conditions continued to deteriorate. Paul traveled to Poland to see if he could find a place for his family to live. Conditions in Poland, however, turned out to be almost as bad as they were in Belarus!

Alex's father felt trapped as he wondered: *How can I care for my family in a place where there's no way to improve our living conditions and government and economic conditions just get worse and worse?*

As he pondered the situation, Paul could think of only one solution: move his family to the United States. That idea raised more questions, however. Would his wife be willing to leave the only home she had ever known? Would they be able to get emigration papers? Would she and the boys be able to make the long trip? Would they adjust to a foreign culture where everyone spoke English? Would they ever see their relatives or homeland again?

When Paul and Natalie discussed the situation, they both felt God was leading them to move. To be eligible to file for emigration papers, however, meant Paul would have to return to the United States.

As his father's departure date neared, Alex, now six, said, "Go and don't worry, Papa. I'll take good care of Mama. I can feed the chickens and bring in the wood for the bake oven."

Paul smiled sadly. He loved his wife and sons as well as his extended family. He wished they could all stay in Belarus! Unfortunately, Paul saw nothing but political turmoil, endless poverty and possible starvation in his native land. Believing emigration was their best option, Paul granted Alex his wish to be the man of the house. In early 1929, with tears streaming down his face, he hugged little Alex warmly, kissed his wife good-bye and set off once again for the United States.

The process of applying for emigration papers took many months. Unable to find steady employment, Paul earned money for his family's trip by doing a variety of odd jobs.

Natalie continued to care for Alex and Nick and to do whatever she could to prepare for the trip. One of her joys was making Alex a sailor suit for the upcoming voyage to America, using a piece of fabric Paul had procured on one of his trips.

Knowing he had never had such fine clothes, Alex wore the little suit whenever he could. One day, while wearing it proudly, an unusually severe thunderstorm hit. In the outhouse when the first thunderbolt exploded, Alex jumped with fright. Holding his pants, he ran for the house, screaming in Russian, *"Bozhenka, Bozhenka, Ya dahm tjebje moy kostium yeslee tih pyerjestahnyesh shoomyet."* ("Dear God, stop making all this noise. I'll give You my suit if only You stop making all this noise!")

Despite her empathy for Alex, Natalie couldn't suppress the gales of laughter that enveloped her as she watched her half-dressed son bolting for the house while bargaining with God. As she held Alex and comforted him, she saw that although he tried to be grown-up in so many ways, he was still a child in his understanding of God.

God's mysterious ways, however, would soon challenge Paul and Natalie's faith as well: Just as it seemed their papers were about to be approved, the Soviet government brought everything to a halt by announcing that no one would be allowed to leave its borders.

Circumstances looked bleak. Paul returned to the emigration office time after time to try to untangle the regulations that thwarted plans to reunite his family. The American officials tried to help but had no authority over their Soviet counterparts.

Uncertainty and helplessness stalked the stalwart couple. Having no idea what their future would be, Paul and Natalie prayed fervently for God's intervention.

After many tries, an American official finally discovered that Paul had initiated the procedure to get his citizenship papers in 1922. "Perhaps Soviet officials will take that into consideration," he suggested, giving Paul a slender glimmer of hope.

Eventually, that glimmer grew into a laser beam that kept the door of emigration open just wide enough to convince authorities to allow the Leonovich family to leave Belarus. The paperwork of seven years earlier, although seemingly insignificant at the time, became a lifelong reminder of God's providence on their behalf.

The Sopli sailor boy welcomed the news with delight and donned his sailor suit with relish. His first boat ride had been daring and dangerous, but it was simply a precursor to future journeys which would involve him in life-changing events around the world.

Faith is the sense of life, that sense by virtue of
which man does not destroy himself, but continues
to live on. It is the force whereby we live.
—Leo Tolstoy, *My Confession*, 1879

CHAPTER 3

LAND OF THE
ENCHANTED FOREST
1929-1935: Belarus to New Jersey

DAWN GENTLY SPREAD HER rosy fingers over the frosty
night as relatives and friends gathered at the
Leonovich cottage to say good-bye. Natalie wept as
she hugged and kissed each person, fearing she would
never see them again.

Alex, dressed in his trusty sailor suit, could hardly
wait for the adventure to begin. Although he said his
farewells dutifully, his mind kept leaping ahead to re-
joining his father in America. His mind danced with
visions of the cars, trucks, trolleys and modern conve-
niences his father had talked about.

Uncle Daniel seemed to sense Alex's excitement
and gave his nephew a special squeeze as he lifted him
onto the horse-drawn wagon that would carry them to
the railroad town of Kobrin. Once he had Alex settled, Daniel loaded their belongings: a dark brown

trunk filled with clothes for the journey and a small bundle of miscellaneous possessions tied together with a square tablecloth.

A few of their closest relatives and Sasha, Alex's favorite playmate, climbed onto the wagon to accompany the little family to Kobrin.

Uncle Daniel gently reminded Natalie that it was time to go and then helped her and baby Nick onto the wagon before climbing up himself. Everyone snuggled down under blankets to keep from shivering as the horse headed to the canal.

At the canal, they got onto a large raft which ferried them across by means of a steel cable. Then, they bounced over the rough roads for two more hours until they reached Kobrin.

In Kobrin, there were more tear-filled good-byes as Alex, his mother and little brother took their seats on the train traveling to Warsaw, Poland. Alex found it difficult to understand why his mother kept crying.

"I'll never see my relatives or homeland again," meant little to the seven-year-old who reveled in the clouds of steam pouring from the smokestack, the roar of the locomotive, the wail of the whistle and the sense of adventure that beckoned him.

The train arrived in Warsaw the following day. Natalie bravely shepherded her little family to the proper pier. Alex's eyes grew wide with wonder when he saw the *S.S. Pilsudski*. The steamship was enormous, and the little sailor who'd launched the rowboat in Sopli sensed that it would take him to a whole new way of life.

The *Pilsudski* took them to Hamburg, Germany, where they picked up additional passengers and freight before sailing to New York City.

Alex loved the salt air and the relentless motion of the sea, but his mother became so seasick she stayed in her berth, caught up in a struggle simply to survive and to care for one-year-old Nick.

That left Alex free to roam the ship. Inquisitive, he watched the crew as they fueled the engines and steered the vessel. Before long, he made friends with the other passengers, some Polish children and the crew who patiently answered his endless questions.

Because his mother was sick, Alex ate alone in the ship's dining room and then carried food back to her and his baby brother.

The days on board ship took on a simple sameness. Finally, after fifteen days at sea, Alex saw people running to the deck. When he joined them, he stared in wonder at the colored lights flashing and flickering on the horizon. "It looks like an enchanted forest!" he exclaimed.

The crew anchored the ship, but disembarkment was slow as the passengers had to be taken in small groups to be processed for immigration. As Alex, Nick and Natalie waited their turn, a welcome tugboat arrived with baskets of fruit which were hoisted up by rope to the passengers on deck.

Alex looked at each piece carefully and then chose a long, curved bright yellow fruit. Never having seen a banana before, he eagerly took a big bite, skin and all. Just as quickly, he spit it out. He had never tasted anything so bitter!

The aftertaste still puckered his mouth as they arrived at Ellis Island. There, Alex got another jolt. He and his mother were separated while they were searched and fumigated. With only a small piece of gauze to hold over his nose, Alex was marched, alone and naked, into a room filled with strong disinfectant. The fumes burned his eyes and nostrils. Scared and humiliated, he felt as if he were being treated like an animal.

Fortunately, when he exited the room, his father was waiting for him. Paul scooped his frightened son into his arms and then helped his family navigate the rest of the details of customs and immigration.

Alex's indignation gradually faded as he and his family rode the ferry to the city. The huge skyscrapers and ships dotting the shore left him breathless. The dancing lights on the theater marquees and billboards mesmerized him as they grew brighter and brighter. And when he saw a maze of cars, trucks, buses and trolleys crawling through paved streets, Alex thought he would burst! Coming from a world of simple cottages, oxen and horses, he found New York City overwhelming and incredible.

Alex also marveled at the people. In Belarus, nearly everyone was fair-skinned, blue-eyed and light-haired.

Here, people came in varied color combinations of skin, eyes and hair. And they were everywhere.

Alex felt as if he were in a fairyland. He wanted desperately to see what was behind the glittering lights and to ride everything that moved, but his father just smiled and shook his head as he loaded his family onto a bus. They would stay with another family for a short time while they adjusted to living in a new land.

When Paul felt his family had learned basic survival techniques, he took them to get settled in their first apartment in Athenia, New Jersey. The apartment had only four rooms, but there were electric lights, an indoor toilet, a big kitchen sink with cold running water and a gas stove, which could also burn wood or coal for heat in the winter. Alex and his mother were delighted.

Luxury ended there, however. None of their dishes or chairs matched. There was no bathtub, which meant showers at the local YWCA each week. No one minded, however, as they no longer needed to walk to the village well or burrow through snow to an outhouse!

Alex began school as soon as they moved in. Although he was seven, he was placed in first grade because he didn't know English. Embarrassed that he couldn't speak the way the others did, he worked very hard in class and also stayed after school for extra help in mastering his new language.

Before long, he understood what people were asking him. Being able to answer questions or converse, however, was more difficult. Unfortunately, many of the children interpreted his silence as being stuck-up, a crime they deemed worthy of ridicule and beatings. Alex's life would have been miserable and quite lonely if Don Balfour, a neighbor and classmate, hadn't befriended and defended Alex in those early days of adjustment.

Many of Alex's teachers also made special efforts to help him overcome the language and cultural differences he faced. With their help, Alex progressed rapidly and was promoted to the third grade the next year, joining those of his own age.

Just two weeks after Alex and his family arrived, however, the American stock market crashed. Banks closed and people panicked. The Great Depression settled in as a time of national tragedy. Life was hard for everyone. For foreigners who didn't know English, however, things were doubly difficult.

Paul tried desperately to get a job, but businesses weren't hiring. In an effort to support his family, he swept floors, washed windows and did odd jobs of every sort.

Natalie began sewing jackets for butchers so she could barter for meat and other supplies. To clothe her children, she patched and re-patched their hand-me-down pants and used bleached flour and sugar sacks to make shirts. She cut around the words and flowers on the sacks as carefully as she could, but a few telltale imprints always managed to peek through. Guessing their source, the other students laughed at Alex and pointed fingers at the "poor Russian immigrant."

Hating ridicule, Alex armed himself with a shoe shine box and stood on street corners and in barbershops offering to shine shoes for two cents. He carefully saved each precious penny so he could buy sneakers and trousers like the other students.

Resources were so scarce that Alex and his father routinely searched for coal along the railroad tracks or picked up branches which had fallen during storms. They felt very fortunate when they found large limbs or whole trees, and used a two-man saw and a homemade wagon to cut and haul the branches home.

Father and son also scoured nearby potato fields for little potatoes which had been overlooked. Natalie used the scrawny potatoes and a few other vegetables to make a variety of meals for her growing family. She stretched the meal with reduced-price stale bread, which she wrapped in a damp towel so she could freshen it by steaming it in the oven.

Conditions in Russia were even worse. That winter, so much snow fell that it came to the tops of the houses. Everything closed. People suffered greatly and many died. Although lonely for their family and homeland, the Leonoviches were grateful to be in America, and as promised, continued to send a package with a few supplies to their relatives every month.

Paul and Natalie's struggle to survive without a steady income stretched out for five years. After a few years, they could no longer afford the rent for their Athenia apartment. Reluctantly, Paul moved his family to a smaller apartment in the poor section of Passaic.

Even though they wanted desperately to be able to be self-sufficient, the Leonoviches learned to graciously accept gifts from others, especially after Elizabeth was born on August 20, 1930.

Nevertheless, they also continued to find ways to help their neighbors and church friends and to send the promised packages back to Belarus until the mid-1930s when Stalin increased his autocratic domination and banned all contact with the United States. Communication of any form between Passaic and Sopli became a game of wits, with mail needing to be coded and sent by way of Poland or Canada.

Despite the difficulties and disappointments, Paul and Natalie refused to give up. Resourceful and hard-working, they determined to rear their children to be obedient and responsible. Because of that, they expected their children to do whatever they were told without complaint.

"If Mother or Dad gave me a scrub bucket, I had to get down on all fours and scrub the floor," Alex recalls. "None of us was allowed to say, 'I don't want to.' "

Alex's parents also banned fighting and rivalry. When the children disagreed, they were expected to work out the problems themselves.

As in most homes, however, principles and actual practice sometimes clashed. For the Leonoviches, the greatest ongoing conflict was over language. Both Paul and Natalie loved their native land and their Slavic heritage. Their constant prayer was for their children to remember their roots and mother tongue so that they would someday be able to help the Russian people. To accomplish that, Natalie refused to learn English and insisted that only Russian be spoken at home. Although bright and outgoing, she even relied on taking the children with her to translate when she went shopping.

Alex, Nick and Betty chafed under these restrictions. They hated being identified as Russians and were determined to do away with every expression or quirk that gave away their background. At times, they whispered together in English at home. If a parent entered the room, they changed to Russian abruptly, hoping they hadn't been heard.

It seldom worked. When caught, they were corrected sharply and instructed, "Speak Russian, children," before being consigned to a corner where they had to kneel without moving.

Trying to maintain ethnic distinctives also led to other conflicts. For Alex, one of the earliest involved radio. From the time he first heard voices coming over a radio in 1931, Alex longed to have one. Since his parents had no money and wouldn't allow English in their home, however, Alex knew better than to ask.

Arthur King, a shoemaker who was a friend of the family, noticed Alex's fascination with radio and made Alex a simple crystal set out of an earphone and crystal.

Alex, suspicious that his parents would be opposed to an antenna going across his bedroom, connected the wire from the crystal set to his bedspring so the springs would act as the needed antenna. Then, earphone over one ear, he moved the cat whisker—a small pointed wire that served as a tuner—around on the crystal until he could hear voices. By careful adjustment, he could pick up two nearby stations, one of which was WAWZ, a pioneer Christian station in Zarephath, New Jersey.

Captivated by the little radio, Alex began going to his room early each evening. After several weeks, his parents slipped into his bedroom to see why Alex kept going to bed so early.

"And what is that?" his mother asked, pointing to the earphone.

"It's a small radio," Alex replied.

"What are you listening to?" she persisted.

"It's a Christian program," Alex told her. Then, grateful there was a hymn she would recognize on WAWZ, he offered to let her listen.

Amazed by the technology and delighted that Alex was listening to gospel programming, his parents decided he could keep the set. Four years later, they saved enough money to buy a small used dome radio, which they placed on the bedroom dresser. Since they could not understand the English programs, however, they conscripted Alex, Nick or Betty to translate.

Leonovich restrictions and idiosyncrasies continually set the family apart as "Russian peasants" even at the Russian Gospel Mission which they attended faithfully. There, the other young people could sit with their friends, but Alex, Nick and Betty were required to sit with their parents. "We were expected to behave or we got it," they remember.

Such strictness sparked an energetic and creative camaraderie between Alex, Nick and Betty, in which they often worked together to achieve privileges, accomplish projects or deflect punishment.

Nick remembers the time he and Alex challenged each other to see who could kick high enough to reach a lightbulb hanging over their beds. Nick eventually won but lost his balance in the process and crashed to the floor. When they heard their father coming to see what was wrong, Alex suggested that they get down on their knees by the bed and pray.

Nick remembers, "Papa stood in the doorway for a little while and finally decided to leave well enough alone and went away. It was years before we told Papa what had really happened."

As the oldest, Alex assumed great responsibility for helping his family in any way he could, using most of his free time to do odd jobs ranging from shining shoes to delivering sales fliers in the tenement houses.

Nick, however, fell in love with football and softball at school. Both boys knew their parents thought sports were worldly and would never consent to Nick's participation. Understanding why Nick wanted to be involved in sports and wishing he could play softball too, Alex became his brother's decoy. When necessary, he made up excuses about Nick's whereabouts. At other times, he tried to get his parents to change their minds by arguing that, after all, sports were mentioned in Scripture.

Over the years, Paul and Natalie softened in their attitude toward sports, eventually adopting a policy of no sports on Sunday rather than no sports at all.

At times, Alex frustrated his parents by doing things of which they disapproved. The most notable was the time he found a discarded cigarette. After hiding behind some bushes where he wouldn't be seen, Alex puffed away.

"Within minutes, I became so sick I decided I would never touch another cigarette," Alex remembers. But when he went home, his mother noticed the smell of smoke and immediately confronted him about it. He vehemently denied smoking, trying every method he knew to convince her. The odor, however, continued to cling to him, destroying all of his eloquent arguments. Denial compounded the problem, resulting in a rare spanking from his father that evening.

At times, Alex's strong will threatened to get the best of his mother. Then, exasperated, she threatened, "If you don't mend your ways, I'm going to pack your bags and send you to a boys' school."

Turbulent times, however, were the exception with the family. Overall, Paul and Natalie mixed frugality, ingenuity and good humor with firmness and hard work to create a well-organized, warm and happy home. They refused to complain about their lot in life, choosing instead to teach their children to cook, sew and embroider so they would have the practical skills they would need throughout life.

Resourcefulness grew out of a philosophy of survival. "Necessity becomes the mother of invention. When nobody could do it, you just had to do it anyway," Alex says.

Life included more than work, however. Alex took violin and clarinet lessons, Nick took trumpet lessons and Betty learned to play the piano and pump organ. Everyone in the family enjoyed singing together.

On Sundays, the Leonoviches attended Russian services at the Russian Gospel Mission in the morning and evening. The children also attended Sunday School at a Brethren Assembly in Passaic in the afternoon. The services lasted several hours, but they included such passion and vitality that the children usually enjoyed them.

Christianity was not just a Sunday affair, however. Scripture reading, prayer and hymn singing permeated their home daily. Natalie was especially known for her ardent praying on behalf of her children.

During the week, the Leonoviches were involved in cottage prayer meetings and youth meetings, often opening their tiny apartment to fifteen or twenty young people. Alex usually played his clarinet or violin as they sang and Natalie, despite their limited resources, always found something for them to eat. Although known as strict Russian peasants with little except God, they always seemed to find something to share with others, even in the depths of the depression.

Finally, in 1934, Paul was called back to work at Botany Worsted Mills. A steady income at last!

The next year, at age thirteen, Alex made a personal commitment to Jesus Christ at a cottage prayer meeting held in their home.

He recalls, "It wasn't an evangelistic service, but I responded because my parents had sown the seed of the gospel and practiced it in their lives. When I saw the sincerity of the other believers praying together, I realized that I needed what they had, and, in the privacy of my room, I knelt and accepted the Lord as my Savior."

Alex's dreams of an enchanted forest and his parents' hopes of economic prosperity, like the banana peel, had a bitter taste to them. Although life punctured their expectations, Alex says, "We were a happy family. My parents generated a spirit of compatibility and love because of their prayers and love. Over and over we saw the Lord provide for our needs. Even though they were strict, they were loving. I owe them a lot and I'm really grateful for their discipline. A person can't give orders until he first learns to take them!"

God does not ask about our ability or our inability,
but our availability.

—*The Arkansas Baptist*

Chapter 4

Full Scholarship or Full Surrender?
1935-1941: Passaic, New Jersey.

"Oh, no. Here come the gospel kids."

Alex and his friends from the Russian Gospel Mission heard that frequently when they were in high school.

"We were Russian and most of them were Polish," Lillian Ladisheff Lubansky, the pastor's daughter, remembers. "We lived on the wrong side of the tracks and went to public school; they were a little better off and went to parochial schools. We went to a little Baptist church while most of them were Catholic. They told us we were going to hell because we didn't go to the right church and that we were overly religious and never had any fun because we didn't go to movies, dances or the local amusement park."

Though she hated the verbal attacks, Lillian remembers those days with delight. The young people from her father's church did not participate in the popular amusements of the day, but they thoroughly enjoyed life—they just did it in different ways. Warm-hearted, outgoing and fun-loving, Alex played a key role in creating the positive dynamic that characterized their times together.

"Alex had a charisma and sense of humor that made everything fun," Lillian recalls. "He was a big guy who was really smart and very good-looking, but he was different from the other kids because he loved the Lord so much. His enthusiasm, boldness and joy were contagious. We elected him president of our youth group because we all looked up to him."

Alex took his leadership role seriously. He often led the twenty young people who gathered around a potbellied stove in robust singing, lively Bible studies and heartfelt prayer sessions. His growing relationship with the Lord brought a vibrant creativity to the weekly meetings.

Getting to know God better and seeing Him answer prayer gave the young people such joy and vitality that they often participated in their church's evangelistic services in Pulasky Park on Sunday afternoons. A large group always gathered as the Russians sang and shared their testimonies. Children climbed trees so they could see and hear better. Alex played his clarinet and Nick his trumpet. Betty played a portable pump organ so everyone could sing. At the end, the younger children gave out tracts and people received an invitation to attend services at the mission church.

Pulasky Park was located behind the housing developments where many of them lived. Other groups, especially the communists, frequently held meetings in another section of the park at the same time in order to distract people. Because the church had secured permission from the city to use amplification, however, their music and testimonies were heard throughout the park, causing one irate communist to threaten the Christians by saying, "When we're in power, you'll be the first to hang from the branches of these trees."

Nothing deterred the Russians in their fervor for the Lord, however, and while seriousness of purpose undergirded both home and church life, so did joy and blessing.

Christmas provided a special opportunity to reach out to a new section of Passaic. While they always caroled to those from their congregation, one year Alex suggested, "Let's go caroling where the rich people live."

No one knew quite what to expect as this was a section of the city they seldom entered. Nevertheless, two dozen young people bundled into their best coats, mittens and scarves and walked to the southeastern part of the city. There, marveling at the beauty of the neighborhood, they strolled from house to house singing the familiar Christmas carols heartily.

Door after door opened as people heard the strong, pure young voices. Time after time they said, "Oh, look, they're the Russian children. Aren't they cute? Don't they sound heavenly?"

Often, the homeowners got tears in their eyes as they listened and many of them gave the young people cash gifts, which they donated to the church treasury.

"You should have seen how big our eyes became the first time someone gave us a $10 bill. That was like being given $100 today," Lillian remembers.

The carolers ended their evening at the Leonovich home, where Alex's mother served them cookies and hot chocolate.

Lillian summarizes it this way: "Everyone knew Alex's family lived by faith, but no matter how much they struggled financially, they always had something to give. And that was never meager! They told us it was because they trusted God and He always provided abundantly."

The simple faith that prompted the Leonoviches to share so joyously also enabled them to find resources to send their children to special conferences to spur them on spiritually.

Most of the other Russian families also saw value in this, so monthly trips to Word of Life rallies at the Gospel Tabernacle in Times Square became the norm. The young people often took the bus to other rallies and conferences in the city as well. Alex frequently helped to organize the trips, which not only provided special opportunities for bonding with each other, but also enlarged the teens' vision of a world beyond their own.

As soon as he was old enough, Alex began working at McCrory's 5 & 10 Cent Store after school. He was assigned to the stockroom where he emptied big cardboard boxes. His coworkers continuously taunted him by saying, "Leonovich, we bet you can't jump inside one of those boxes."

Finally Alex decided, "I had to prove them wrong, so I jumped into a box."

As soon as he did, the other workers put the lid on the box.

Just then the manager walked in. "Are the boxes empty?" he asked. "The truck's outside to pick up the cartons."

Alex thought to himself, *Leonovich, now you've done it. How are you going to explain to your parents that you lost your job?*

Alex listened as the manager came closer and closer, kicking each box before saying, "Dump it."

As he squatted in the box fearing the worst, Alex thought, *I'll be fired anyway, so I might as well have some fun.*

When Alex felt the manager's hand on his box, he jumped up. The manager's face blanched and he looked as if he might fall over, but then surprise gave way to laughter and he said, "Leonovich, you pulled a good one on me." Alex joined in the laughter, grateful to still have his job.

Long before he started working at McCrory's, Alex determined he would buy his mother a washing machine as soon as he got a steady job. He hated seeing her raw, bleeding knuckles from scrubbing clothes on a washboard. Later, he enlisted Betty to save what she earned so they could also purchase a refrigerator for the family.

Practical as he was, however, Alex also understood a woman's need for beauty and occasionally surprised his mother with fresh flowers. She always protested, saying they needed the money for more important things, but Alex knew that she was secretly delighted.

Regardless of their outside responsibilities, Alex, Nick and Betty were always expected to help at home, do well in school and practice their musical instruments faithfully. They also sang together, eventually forming a trio which traveled to area churches to sing and share what God was doing in their lives.

When Alex was seventeen, his mother gave birth to Peter, the last of the Leonovich children. Born on June 16, 1940, little Peter brought the usual assortment of new joys and challenges.

In 1941 Alex graduated from high school with top honors. Fascinated with machines and technology ever since he could remember, he was thrilled when he was awarded a full scholarship in engineering to Butler University in Indiana.

His parents were exuberant. The scholarship was one of only three such scholarships awarded by the state of New Jersey, and they saw this as an almost miraculous opportunity for Alex to acquire the college education they couldn't afford. Excited and proud, Alex looked forward to a good career where he could use his earnings to help his parents and to support missionaries around the world.

Alex continued to work at McCrory's after graduation. In addition, he led the young people's group at his church and taught a Sunday school class in the back of a Salvation Army storefront in Passaic.

War clouds rumbled repeatedly. On June 22, 1941, Germany invaded Russia, ushering in great devastation and loss of life. As it had done for the other allied nations, the United States sent aid to ease the suffering but refused to involve itself by sending troops.

That July, Alex attended a missionary conference in Chicago. Peter Deyneka, Sr., sometimes called "Peter Dynamite," spoke about total surrender. Deep within, Alex felt a titanic tug-of-war begin as he felt God calling him to full-time missionary service.

"You allowed me to earn the scholarship, and You know how much I would enjoy a career in science. Besides, I promise to use it wisely by helping my family and supporting many missionaries," Alex told the Lord.

Unfortunately, no matter how eloquent his arguments, he still felt miserable. The turmoil soon showed on his usually happy face.

Peter Deyneka happened to know Alex since his wife, Vera, was related to Alex's mother. Sensing something was wrong, Deyneka called Alex aside. "Alex, where's your smile?" he asked.

Alex didn't want to tell him what the problem was, but finally admitted, "I think God wants me to be a missionary to the Russian people, but I just earned a full scholarship to Butler University and I'd really like to be an engineer. Besides, if I turn down the scholarship, I won't be able to go to college because my family can't afford it."

Deyneka suggested that they pray. Alex didn't want to. He knew what would happen if they prayed, and he really didn't want to give up his opportunity to get an education.

Deyneka persisted. Finally he persuaded Alex to go to an upper room with him. There, in his broken Russian-English, Peter prayed fervently that God would speak to Alex so that he would surrender to the Lord. When he finished, he said, "Now, Alex, you pray."

Alex hesitated. Then, reluctantly, he started praying. "At first my prayer was just words," he remembers. "But then the Lord broke my heart and spirit. Tears flowed down my cheeks as I said with a contrite heart, 'Father, not my will but Thine be done.' "

As Alex surrendered his treasured scholarship, God's peace welled up within him and his smile returned. From then on, the conference filled him with joy and excitement as he searched for God's guidance. He returned home filled with enthusiasm. His parents, however, even after years of praying that their children would serve the Lord, could not understand.

"How can you give up four years of education? We saw your scholarship as a gift from God," Alex's father said sadly. Then he added, "We won't stand in your way, Alex, if this is how God is leading, but all we can do is pray that the Lord will somehow provide for you because we can't do anything."

Alex knew that was true; his father was earning only $15-$18 a week. With no idea how he would pay for an education or where he should go, Alex sent inquiries to a number of Bible schools and colleges. The only one to offer him admission on such short notice was Nyack Missionary Training Institute in Nyack, New York. Alex filled out his application papers just a few weeks before the fall term was to begin.

"All you need is $80 for registration and you can be enrolled," he was told.

"At that time, I didn't even have 80 cents, so I just committed it to the Lord and continued teaching in the Salvation Army storefront mission in Passaic," Alex remembers.

"One evening I came home to the tenement building where I lived. I looked at the row of mailboxes out of habit. Through the peephole in our mailbox, I saw something that looked like a white envelope. I quickly opened the mailbox and found a special delivery letter from some friends.

"When I opened it, I read, 'Alex, we heard that you were planning to go to Bible school. God laid it on our hearts to send you the enclosed gift.'

"I looked at the check. And would you believe it was $80 to the penny? Not a penny more; not a penny less. I knew this was God's clear approval and provision, so I accepted the gift with gratitude and hitch-hiked to Nyack. After I paid my registration, I asked where I could find employment.

"I was directed to the 9W Diner in Nyack, where I was hired on the spot as a short-order cook and dishwasher. For the next four years, I worked from 11 p.m. until 6 a.m. and attended classes and studied from 8 in the morning until 2 in the afternoon. After lunch, I rested for four or five hours and then studied for two or three hours before going back to work. The hours were long and the work tiring, but I knew that was what God wanted . . . so I just did it."

Love is never lost. If not reciprocated, it will flow
back and soften and purify the heart.

—Washington Irving

CHAPTER 5

"I'LL NEVER MARRY A GREENHORN!"

1941-1945: Nyack, New York; Canada.

IN THE FALL OF Alex's second year at Nyack, Dr. Lee
Olsen, Professor of Music, approached Alex and said,
"Leonovich, there's a Russian choir coming to record
some songs. You're Russian, so why don't you serve as
host to the group? Just show them around and answer
any questions they have."

"That's fine with me," Alex replied, intrigued by
the idea, especially when he discovered that choirs
from the Freehold and South River Russian churches
had been organized into one large choir so that Peter
Deyneka could use the music on his Russian broadcasts over radio station HCJB in Quito, Ecuador.

The day the choir was scheduled to arrive, Alex
and his friend, Ray Bridgham, waited near a win-
dow in a classroom on the second floor of Beracca,
the music building which housed the recording studios.

As the afternoon faded into evening, a caravan of six cars drove into the parking lot. Alex's excitement at seeing thirty Russian young people get out of the cars escalated when he noticed a beautiful blonde wearing a bright red dress. He elbowed Ray and said, "If there's a girl I marry, it's going to be her."

Then he flashed Ray a big smile and hurried off to greet the group.

And to meet the girl in red.

For Alex, the bells of romance rang loud and clear as he showed the choir around and set up microphones for the recording session. He knew his time was limited and so used every opportunity to learn what he could about the girl who had captured his heart.

Alex still remembers the occasion vividly and says, "Babs thought I was nervy because I wanted to know her name right away. When I found out that her brothers were in the choir, I became real friendly with them so that I could have a point of access. I told them I'd like to come visit them, but my real purpose was to get to know Babs better. Of course, at that time, I didn't realize she had told her mother she would never marry a Russian."

◊ ◊ ◊ ◊ ◊ ◊ ◊

If Babs had ever been clear about anything, it was that she was not going to marry a Russian. Tired of being shunned and ridiculed by neighbors and class-

mates who thought that all Russians were either unso-
phisticated immigrants or dangerous communists,
Babs adopted one of their derogatory nicknames for
immigrants and asserted repeatedly throughout her
high school years, "I'll never marry a Greenhorn."

The lively young lady with a mind of her own had
been born in South River, New Jersey, on March 8,
1923. She was christened Mary Babich and frequently called Manechka, Manya or Maria as a child,
which was good because she always hated the name
Mary. In high school, using last names became
trendy. Before long, Babich was shortened to Babs,
"the name you'll use if you're my friend," she'd say.

Babs's parents grew up near Minsk, Belarus. Her
father, Sedor Babich, moved to America in 1914 and
worked for the Hercules Company until he was
drafted into the infantry of the United States Army
during World War I. He eventually met and married
Julia Shilinin. Both were Christians who had come to
know the Lord through friends.

The oldest of three children, Babs remembers her
parents as devout, loving, outgoing people who made
their home a happy place, always keeping it open to
others, especially visiting ministers.

Sedor and Julia spoke Russian at home but allowed
their children to speak English. As a result, despite
her exposure to Russian at home and in the church,
Babs did not learn to read or write her parents' language until after she started singing in the Russian

choir when she was eleven. The director insisted that they learn the pronunciation of the words by repeating after him. As she followed along in her music, Babs gradually learned to read Russian.

"It wasn't really that hard because in Russian you pronounce every letter," she says.

Overall, however, neither Babs nor her brothers were interested in their Russian heritage. Having been born in America, they wanted to be completely American. Furthermore, their relatives in the Soviet Union had severed all ties, saying, "Don't contact us" because they feared they would lose their government jobs.

Babs became a Christian in her early teens and, despite her eagerness to eliminate all evidence of her Russian background, forged a strong friendship with Nadine, a fellow Russian Christian. They believed they were the only Christians in their high school, so they did their best to please the Lord.

The Babiches and several other families from their church frequently attended the regional RUEBU conferences where Babs and Nadine often sang duets. As they traveled to cities such as Buffalo, Hartford, Detroit, Philadelphia, Bethlehem and Wilkes-Barre, Pennsylvania, Babs's father treated Babs as his chief navigator by having her read the maps, a skill she would use throughout life.

Babs enjoyed singing at the conferences, but she recoiled at the thought of going into full-time Christian service. In particular, she was opposed to the idea of being a preacher's wife, especially if he were Russian!

Lighthearted and full of fun, Babs had a way of quietly bringing joy wherever she went. Meeting Alex on her trip to Nyack, however, unnerved her. He was handsome, smart and witty. His love for the Lord, for the Russian people and for her burned intensely. Too intensely.

Why had he fallen in love with her when he didn't even know her? And now, what should she do? He was certainly intelligent and persuasive, but if she let herself fall in love with him, she would end up being a Russian preacher's wife—the one thing she was determined not to do. On the other hand . . .

◊ ◊ ◊ ◊ ◊ ◊ ◊

Deferred from military service because he was a ministerial student, Alex already had a full schedule of classes, work and ministry when Babs set his heart racing. Although he and his friends, Paul Freed, Ben Armstrong and Tom Mosley, had enjoyed dating several of the girls at Nyack, Alex knew immediately that Babs would hold a special place in his life.

For their first date, Alex invited Babs to "Missions In Review," an annual musical production staged by Nyack's orchestra and choirs at Carnegie Hall. Complete with costumes, the event was the highlight of the school year and the hall was always packed. Babs accepted his invitation to the black-tie affair and was enthralled. She had never been to Carnegie Hall nor to such an elaborate production before. Dating a Russian preacher boy was certainly different than she had imagined!

The early days of Alex's pursuit of Babs took place in a 1929 navy Studebaker with wooden spoke wheels. Alex's father had bought the car from a neighbor for $25 and given it to him during his first year at Nyack. An enormous, unwieldy vehicle which had to be backed up and turned a second time before negotiating sharp right turns, it was quickly nicknamed "Noah's Ark" by Alex's college cohorts. Now, whenever he could, Alex drove the Ark to Babs's home in South River to get to know her and her family better.

The Ark also played a vital part in Alex's ministry—until one night when he was taking the teens to Nyack for a special program. With the car packed with young people, one of the tires gave out. Alex stopped and changed the tire, but he had no sooner started driving again when the spare also went flat. Since the car had a spare tire by each wheel, Alex simply changed the second flat. But when the same thing happened three more times, Alex ran out of tires and had to call the police to take him and the other young people home.

Unable to afford new tires, Alex sold Noah's Ark for $10. Gus Gaetjen, a good-hearted Christian gas station owner, found an inexpensive 1935 blue Plymouth for Alex. It became the primary car in which Alex courted Babs.

The Plymouth had one major problem: It was an oil guzzler. Gus was constantly giving Alex five-gallon cans of used drain oil to replenish the ever-diminishing oil supply.

The Plymouth sported a canvas roof. Unfortunately, it leaked. Babs soon showed her sense of humor and ability to adjust by using an umbrella inside the car so she could keep from getting soaked when it rained.

Although attracted to Alex, Babs continued to struggle with the idea of marrying a Russian preacher. Convinced of his love for Babs, Alex simply surrounded her with love and, as his father had done with him, waited for her to reciprocate. He understood her doubts about being involved in full-time ministry but knew he could not abandon his promise to the Lord.

Alex's calling was reconfirmed by Mary Selody, a missionary who ran an orphanage in Carpathia, Russia. As he shared his vision of being a missionary to the Slavic world at a local Russian-Ukrainian church, Miss Selody slipped him a $100 bill and said, "May the Lord encourage you. And don't ever stop doing what God calls you to do." Her words inspired Alex and her generous gift brought tears to his eyes. She had many needs, he knew, and had given out of love rather than abundance.

Alex's willingness to go anywhere and do anything was tested during the summers of 1943 and 1944 when

Canadian Christians invited him to take the gospel to the Doukhobors, a Russian religious sect which had split from the Russian Orthodox Church in 1785. Believing they were struggling against the Holy Spirit because they opposed the use of icons and what they called the "idolization of the Bible," Archbishop Ambrosius referred to them as *"Doukho-bortsi,"* meaning "Spirit-wrestlers." The group accepted the name, claiming to wrestle with and for the Spirit of God.

In the beginning, they held biblical standards. But as they added to Scripture, their beliefs became corrupted so that they began to see God merely as a spiritual force of goodness and creativity and the soul of a person as the reflection of God's Spirit in that person. Their philosophy rested on loving God and your neighbor as expressed in their Book of Life, made up of psalms for memorization.

Considered rebels against the Orthodox Church, many of the Doukhobors were persecuted and exiled to the Caucasus Mountains throughout the 1800s. In 1895, under the leadership of Peter Vasilievitch Verigin, known as Peter the Lordly, the Doukhobors burned arms and weapons and refused to eat meat in a decisive stand against all forms of militarism and violence. In response, the Czarist state and the Orthodox Church increased their persecution until the Doukhobors' plight attracted worldwide attention and led to their migration to western Canada in 1899.

In the early part of the twentieth century, the Doukhobors lived together in close-knit agrarian communities of about twenty families each. Their standards deteriorated under the leadership of Peter Petrovich Verigin, known as Peter the Cleaner, because he gambled away their tax money, had sexual relations with the women and drank excessively under the pretense of "taking the sins" of the community.

By the time Alex arrived, many of the Doukhobors were fanatics who lived in communes where free love was practiced. They were also strict vegetarians refusing to kill anything, even flies.

Canadian Christians had tried to reach some of the Doukhobor communities but felt that because Alex spoke their language, he would have a greater impact. They were right. The Doukhobors were amazed that someone who was an American could speak such fluent Russian. They also marveled at Alex's demonstration of love, which was so great that it broke down their defenses.

Alex traveled from commune to commune, preaching and offering to set up Vacation Bible Schools because he found the people responded better to children's programs. As soon as some of the boys and girls showed interest in the gospel, he helped organize Sunday schools so they could continue to learn about God.

By the next year, some of the adults told of coming to know the Lord because of the changes they'd seen in the young people.

But tensions were mounting. Many of the Doukhobors had become radicals known as Sons of Freedom. They continuously blew up schools because they didn't want their children to get a "devilish education."

They also practiced promiscuity, justifying it by saying, "The Spirit tells me you should be my spiritual wife."

Those living near their commune grew tired of the explosions and immoral lifestyle and decided to retaliate by blowing up the marble vault where Peter Verigin was buried. When the explosion went off, it was so large that it broke windows in Castlegar, eighteen miles away.

Horrified, the Doukhobors gathered to protest. Their method? Hundreds lined up, dropped their clothes and prepared to march into the town of Brilliant nude. Just as they were ready to leave, someone shouted "Fire Brigade!"

Pandemonium broke out. While the Doukhobors knew the water wouldn't kill them, they feared the searing pain of the pressurized water from the fire hoses. Utter confusion reigned as they struggled to find their own clothes, a monumental task since everyone wore similar things in different sizes.

Not long after the episode in Brilliant, Alex went to a village he'd never visited before. Suddenly, he found himself surrounded by a circle of hefty naked women who said, "Let's do the same thing to him that we did to the tax collector."

Alex quickly recalled that this group had forcibly stripped the tax collector of his clothes so that he barely escaped with his undershorts on. Not interested in a repeat performance, Alex cried, "Help, Lord!" and then shouted to his partner, "Let's get out of here." With the women momentarily distracted by his shouts, Alex broke through their circle. He and his Canadian companion grabbed their bikes and pedaled wildly.

Despite all of the problems, many children and several adults seemed genuinely grateful that Alex had come. One elderly woman said, "You said Christ was coming back, not Peter Verigin. Show me."

As Alex explained what the Bible said, she asked, "If that's the truth, why haven't others come before to show us the truth?"

Another woman responded to his invitation for salvation. Then she said, "So many of our families have lived and died without hearing. Why didn't someone come sooner?"

Alex's summer work eventually led to follow-up ministry and a radio outreach by Canadian Christians, but the questions about coming sooner would haunt him the rest of his life.

◊ ◊ ◊ ◊ ◊ ◊ ◊

Alex graduated from Nyack in 1944 but decided to stay for another year of graduate work. Work, study and ministry filled his days . . . and nights.

By then, Babs had seen Alex in a wide variety of situations. There was no doubt that marrying him would mean involvement in Russian ministry, but the longer she knew Alex, the more her objections melted away.

"Alex knocked away the stereotypes I had formed in my mind about marrying a Russian or being a preacher's wife," Babs says. "Besides, my mother kept holding a shotgun at my head! And, most importantly, I started looking for God's will instead of my own."

As Babs began to reciprocate Alex's love, he sensed the change and sought extra jobs so he could buy her an engagement ring. One evening, while on his way to speak at the National Tabernacle in Washington, D. C., he stopped at her home.

"That night when Babs left the room, I asked her mother and father for their consent and blessing in asking Babs to marry me. Although I thought they would respond in the affirmative, it was beautiful to hear them say they were praying this would happen.

"I waited until Babs returned and then watched from a distance as she stood in front of a mirror to put her hair up in curlers for the night. I walked over to her and told her how much I loved her. Her eyes filled with tears and she embraced me.

"Then I added, 'You know, I'm in college and am not prepared to give you an engagement ring right now. I hope I can do that at some future time. Would you accept me as I am with just a wedding band?'

"Babs replied, 'Yes, I understand,' and we both knelt in prayer. Holding each other's hands, we committed ourselves to loving the Lord first and each other second."

Alex stopped in at Babs's home again several days later. After visiting for a while, he tossed her something wrapped in newspaper, saying, "Just a little souvenir."

When she opened the wrapping, she found a diamond ring. She knew how hard it was for Alex to work his way through school, and she began to cry.

Sensing that his life would be full of challenges and uncertainties and that anyone who married him would have to be ready for anything, Alex felt he needed to be sure that Babs could do that.

She passed the test brilliantly.

That same year, Peter Deyneka, Sr., contacted Alex to ask if he would go to HCJB to expand their Russian programming. Alex agreed to give it a try as soon as he completed his year at Nyack.

That May, as they celebrated Alex's graduation, the young couple joined the nation in also celebrating Germany's surrender to the Allies. Although the war in the Pacific remained unresolved, a general feeling of hope and optimism permeated the country as Alex prepared to leave for South America.

On Memorial Day weekend in 1945, Babs and his parents took Alex to the New York's Grace Line Pier.

Just before his departure for Quito, Ecuador, his mother read Second Timothy 2:1-3:

> Thou therefore, my son, be strong in the grace that is in Christ Jesus. And the things that thou hast heard of me among many witnesses, the same commit thou to faithful men, who shall be able to teach others also. Thou therefore endure hardness, as a good soldier of Jesus Christ.

Then, amidst tear-filled embraces, Alex bid his beloved fiancée and parents farewell and left for Ecuador.

He who labors as he prays lifts his heart to God with his hands.

—St. Bernard of Clairvaux

CHAPTER 6

EVEN GOD CAN'T STEER A PARKED CAR

1945-1947: South America

"WORLD WAR II IS over! Japan has unconditionally surrendered to the American forces!"

The news flash interrupted Alex's thoughts as he watched the second hand count off the final moments before he was to go on the air with "New Life," his daily Russian short-wave program. Exhilarated, he thought, *Dear Lord, what a wonderful way to begin the program!*

The second hand reached twelve. Alex's "On The Air" light flashed and his microphone went live.

Alex tried to picture those who might be listening. Then, abandoning his intended message, he spoke fervently in his native tongue, "Friends, this afternoon I wish to speak from my heart to yours about unconditional surrender to Jesus Christ."

His voice crackled along static-filled, shortwave signals all the way from his studio at radio station

HCJB in Quito, Ecuador, back to Passaic, New Jersey, where his mother sat listening to the program. Her eyes were closed so she could concentrate better when Alex's sixteen-year-old brother, Nick, walked into the room.

Normally Nick would have stalked out. He thought his family was way too religious. After all, who needed religion when you had great friends like he did?

That day, however, Nick dropped his books and sat down. Partway through the program, his mother heard a sound and opened her eyes. Huge tears were rolling down Nick's face and splashing on the linoleum. When their eyes met, he started sobbing. "*Mamochka*," he said, kneeling by the radio, "Please pray with me. I want to dedicate my life to the Lord just like Alex."

When Alex heard what had happened, he took it as an affirmation of God's call to broadcast in the Russian language. His brother had surrendered his life to the Lord!

◊ ◊ ◊ ◊ ◊ ◊ ◊

Alex had seen AM radio grow popular in the United States during the war, but his mission was to penetrate the Soviet Union with the gospel by shortwave, a plan which was almost without precedent. He had no idea how the project would be financed or whether it would be effective. The idea of sitting in a studio high in the Andes Mountains of

Quito, Ecuador, in order to speak to the people of the Soviet Union seemed incredible.

The communists were known for jamming unwanted radio signals; they had banned shortwave transmission and stated that anyone caught with a radio would be considered a foreign agent. Alex understood why people shook their heads with hesitant skepticism and asked, "Who will listen? They don't even have radios."

Having seized power over twenty years earlier, Josef Stalin controlled both the Communist Party and the Russian government. Known for shrewdness and ruthlessness, he was at the height of his power. Internal purges and military victories allowed him autocratic rule over the millions of people living under the banner of the hammer and sickle. How could invisible radio signals ever hope to penetrate Stalin's seemingly impregnable barricade to outside influence—that intimidating Soviet isolationism later known as the Iron Curtain?

Four years before Alex's arrival, in March 1941, Peter Deyneka, Sr., General Director of the Russian Gospel Association (RGA, later named the Slavic Gospel Association), had visited his friends, Clarence Jones and Reuben Larsen, co-founders of HCJB. They invited Deyneka to do some live broadcasts in English and then said, "Peter, let's try broadcasting in Russian and see if anyone listens."

Knowing there were large colonies of Slavic people who had settled in South America in the 1920s in response to government offers of land, HCJB personnel aimed the short-wave signal south into those countries. The Slavs responded immediately.

When Deyneka returned to the United States, he began using a disc-cutting machine to record fifteen-minute programs to send to HCJB. The programs were aired weekly beginning on June 22, 1941. Several months later, Deyneka began producing two programs a week.

By late 1942, RGA staff members were sent to HCJB to produce live Russian broadcasts. Over the next few years, HCJB's engineering staff worked diligently to develop technology to penetrate the Soviet Union. Their efforts led to the cubicle quad antenna, hailed as a major breakthrough because it allowed the station to boost and target power.

Alex was thrilled with the potential, but frustrated with his lack of experience. When he arrived, he was asked to work as an announcer and engineer because the radio station was short-staffed. Knowing nothing about broadcasting, Alex spent his first weeks learning how to operate the equipment. At the same time, he prayed constantly for guidance about the format, music and messages to use for his programs.

Alex's commitment to excellence started him on a search for music which would impact listeners. He soon learned why Deyneka had arranged for the Russian choir to make recordings at Nyack: Recorded Russian gospel music was almost nonexistent! To

solve the problem, Alex recruited HCJB pianists
Wilda Savage and Janice Terwilliger to accompany
him while he made recordings.

Recording, however, was a major project in those pioneer days of radio, especially when music was involved.
The process required using a disc-cutting machine to cut
grooves into a fifteen inch enamel-covered metal disc
with a needle. Tedious and time-consuming, it required
great patience and precision. Any mistake by the engineer, musicians or speaker meant starting over with a
new disc. All through the session, an engineer had to
make sure that none of the fine enamel hairs being cut
from the disc fell where they would disrupt the recording. Afterward, great care had to be taken in cleaning up
the shiny black strands.

Producing recordings, however, was not the only
problem. Alex also had trouble finding appropriate
music to record. In order to use some of the great music of the day along with the old hymns, Alex began
translating pieces like "Ninety and Nine" and "The
Holy City" into Russian. Many of his translations
were later included in Russian hymnals published in
South America.

When Alex launched the premier edition of "New
Life" on July 23, 1945, it reverberated with joy and enthusiasm as he sang and spoke words of encouragement.
Always hoping that the Russian people would find some
way to listen, Alex threw himself into the work of producing daily fifteen-minute broadcasts. The only one in

the world broadcasting gospel programs in Russian at that time, he took the responsibility seriously.

Unfortunately, HCJB still needed him to work regular shifts in addition to his Russian broadcasts. Alex was often forced to plan "New Life" while airing other programs. Somehow, he also managed to find the time to identify and catalogue programs and platters and set up a system for handling correspondence.

Intrigued by radio since the crystal-set days of his youth, Alex believed in its power. His goal, however, was not merely to penetrate Soviet airwaves but to reach Russian hearts. Continuing to do that on an ongoing basis required stamina and courage.

Shortwave transmissions could, and would, be picked up by friend and foe alike, and Soviet officials had made their opposition to Christianity very clear. Alex knew the risks of becoming the voice identified with the gospel: It could further jeopardize the safety of his relatives still living in the Soviet Union and could make him and his family targets of communist harassment in America.

Furthermore, there was no way to assess the effectiveness of the programs in the USSR. Even if people found a way to listen, they would be unable to respond because they were forbidden to make contact with the West. Preparing the programs would be a lonely experience of faith.

Still, Alex felt God's call to do this. He'd always told the Passaic young people, "You never know what you can do until you try. If you don't attempt it, you won't accomplish it. It's better to fail than to not try. The good Samaritan simply did what he could. Get involved, even if it's with menial tasks. Remember, even God can't steer a parked car."

Never one to preach what he would not practice, Alex accepted the challenge even while feeling a great sense of inadequacy. He looked to the Lord constantly. "I never knew anything about radio ministry, but the Lord allowed me to develop it as a means of communicating the gospel. Instead of thinking that thousands might be listening, I tried to visualize just one individual to whom I might be speaking. I tried to make it very personal so each person would feel as though the message was directed to him personally."

Alex longed for at least one letter or postcard from the USSR to indicate that people were listening. Was the signal getting through? Was it clear? Did people have radios? Could they listen? Did they understand what he was saying? Would they respond to the gospel? Month after month, however, he heard nothing from the Soviet Union.

Encouragement to keep going came instead from the Slavs who had settled in South America. Once poor countries with huge dense forests, Argentina, Paraguay, Uruguay, Venezuela and Brazil had recruited Poles, Ukrainians and Russians to turn the jungles into farms. Promised free land if they cultivated it, the Slavs now numbered 5 million. Many of them responded enthusiastically to Alex's program and asked him to hold meetings in their communities.

When Alex spoke to these Russian congregations, revival often broke out and many people came to know the Lord. At times, however, that sparked trouble.

"One woman's husband became very upset when she chose to be a Christian because she had been his drinking buddy," Alex recalls. "He decided to get rid of the man who had changed his wife, so he got his handgun, drank enough liquor to get really drunk and came to the burlap tent where we were meeting.

"Instead of shooting me, however, he fell asleep because he was so drunk. When he woke up, he was totally embarrassed. Later, he too became a believer."

Some of Alex's invitations took him to remote villages where people still lived in mud huts and traveled by horse and wagon. Alex thought of his childhood days in Belarus as he bumped along. When rain turned the red clay into mud so slippery that the horses couldn't keep their footing, sure-footed oxen who pulled *sulkas* at a rate of about a mile and a half an hour became the only means of transportation.

Many of the groups Alex visited in the primitive rain forests clung to ultraconservative ways. For them, life remained as rugged as it had been when they arrived in the 1920s. Still wielding machetes and shovels to clear the untamed jungles, they lived simple lives vulnerable to the intense heat and tropical diseases that had killed thousands of Slavic immigrants.

Having Alex come for meetings meant placing boards over the stumps of trees to serve as benches and setting up a table on a back porch for a pulpit. The older people were astounded by, and sometimes critical of, the many young people who responded to the gospel because they had been taught that religion was only for adults.

Most people, however, welcomed Alex and his colleague, Emilio Ziatko, a Russian who spoke fluent Spanish. Families eagerly invited the missionaries to eat with them, frequently an exciting, unpredictable experience.

Always appreciative and gracious, Alex accepted whatever his hosts offered him. At times, that meant drinking from a common gourd, using the same metal straw to strain out tea leaves as a man with saliva dripping off his beard or drinking warm goat's milk from a cup wiped out with a dirty apron after the woman had spit into the cup to clean it.

Once Alex stayed in a tiny one-room adobe house with only one bed and a bench. When it came time for bed, the host said, "You're going to share the bed with my wife."

"No, no, you'll sleep in bed with your own wife," Alex objected. "I'll sleep on the bench."

Trying to be hospitable and with no thought of impropriety, the man persisted. Alex remained adamant.

Finally the man agreed and went outside to get some straw which he laid on the bench. Then, to assure Alex's comfort, he covered the straw with a piece of cowhide.

Despite his virtuous stand, however, Alex got no sleep that night—the cowhide was full of fleas! When morning finally came, his body was covered with flea bites, resembling an outbreak of measles.

Another time a family served him fried worms. "They looked like spaghetti," Alex remembers. "The people were being kind and giving me the best they had to offer. How could I refuse? Besides, if I had, they would never have called me back."

On one occasion, however, even Alex couldn't bring himself to eat what was served. "The barbecued monkey meat looked too much like a baby and I just couldn't eat it."

Pork also became a problem. "Pork was such a special treat to them that many families served it when they had special company. I remember one night when a family killed a piglet in my honor. I ate it even though I knew I would regret it. That time, however, I became deathly ill. The constant diet of pork almost did me in . . . . They almost killed me with pork love."

Alex's willingness to sacrifice himself opened doors that would not have opened in any other way, but it took its toll. One day he became extremely tired and discouraged as he was riding in a wagon pulled by a team of oxen. Lonely, he asked, "What am I doing here?" As he began to feel sorry for himself, he heard some women in the tea fields sing,

> I know the Lord will make a way for me
> If I trust and never doubt,
> The Lord will surely bring me out.

Alex perked up. He had used the chorus on the radio and taught it in the villages! "The Lord reversed the flow of ministry and used the song I'd taught others to help me. Suddenly I felt rejuvenated and went on my way rejoicing," Alex remembers.

At times Alex resorted to his God-given sense of humor as a stress reliever and spirit-lifter. Members of the HCJB staff often had breakfast together at Clarence Jones' home. One morning, Alex decided to have some fun as they were eating.

Knowing native people who kept a boa constrictor as a pet, he decided to borrow it. Alex got up early, went to their home, draped the snake around his neck, put his coat over it and joined the staff for breakfast. Before long, he announced, "It's awfully hot in here," and took off his jacket.

Suddenly there were shrieks and shouts, and Alex had the table all to himself. "No one was hurt and it was just clean fun," Alex says.

Whether everyone else agreed is still not certain, but chances are good that everyone laughed about the incident later, because Alex's commitment to the Lord, dedication to hard work and abundant love for others encouraged everyone on the staff. His mother's send-off passage from Second Timothy 2:3, about enduring hardness as a good soldier of Jesus Christ so characterized his life that it appeared next to his photo in the fourteenth anniversary issue of *Call of the Andes*.

Alex gave himself wholeheartedly to reaching the Russian people with the gospel, but his pace was so hectic that his health broke. In January 1947, Alex passed out as he started speaking to a group in a remote village. As he looked at those sitting on the tree stumps, everything began turning inside his head. As he started to fall toward the makeshift pulpit on the porch, some of the men caught him and took him inside to a bed.

Alex says, "When I awoke, water was trickling down my face. They called the doctor in that city and he said: 'If you hadn't begun to cry, you might have become a vegetable. Those tears were God's safety valve to relieve the pressure.' "

The doctor felt Alex was on the verge of a nervous breakdown from the intensity of his schedule and the constant changes of altitude, temperature, diet and lifestyle from journeying back and forth between the mountains and the jungles. He ordered Alex to return to the United States.

Being forced to leave South America after only nineteen months disappointed Alex greatly. He had led people to the Lord through his radio broadcasts and evangelistic meetings and had established mission stations, but he had made only a small dent in the overwhelming need. Why had God allowed him to stall out in the midst of such important work?

It is love that asks, that seeks, that knocks, that
finds, and that is faithful to what it finds.

—St. Augustine

CHAPTER 7

WITH EVERY PETAL
1945-1948: Toronto, Canada;
United States

WHILE ALEX MINISTERED IN South America, Babs at-
tended the Russian Bible Institute at the People's
Church in Toronto, Canada, where Dr. Oswald J.
Smith was the pastor.

She studied in the morning and then worked as a
secretary at Barclay's Direct By Mail Service in the
afternoon. In the evenings, she attended choir practice, participated in prayer meetings or traveled
with the Melody Girls' Trio. The trio, along with
other musicians, traveled with Dr. Smith's son,
Paul, as he preached throughout Ontario on week-
ends.

Babs thoroughly enjoyed studying, traveling with
the team and exploring Toronto. She and her new
friends took trolleys to the department stores where
they reveled in shopping and sampling dishes like fish
'n chips and Boston creme pie.

Separated by many miles, Alex and Babs tried to stay in touch by letter. Babs says, "Alex wrote frequently. I didn't have as much to say, but I tried to write almost every day too."

Ever ingenious, Alex included coded words and songs for Babs as he prepared his radio broadcasts. Both dreamed of the day Babs would travel to Quito so they could get married.

Babs completed her studies in May 1946. Mrs. Oswald Smith honored Babs with a graduation tea, complete with beautiful bone china teacups. Sensing Babs's delight with the china cups, Mrs. Smith gave Babs her first teacup and saucer as a going-away gift when she finished working in June.

With happy memories of her time in Canada, Babs packed her belongings and moved back to her parents' home in New Jersey. There she found a job as a secretary for Templar Oil Company, reactivated her former friendships and activities and busied herself with wedding preparations.

While getting ready to go to a special youth conference in January 1947, she received the surprise of her life.

Ordered home because of medical problems, Alex had booked passage on the first freighter he could find. When he landed in Wilmington, Delaware, he took a train to New Brunswick, New Jersey. Then he boarded a bus for South River where he eagerly knocked on Babs's door.

Seeing the thin, mustached man whom she thought was in Ecuador caught Babs completely off guard and she blurted out, "What am I to do now? I was just getting ready to go to a special young people's conference in Philadelphia."

Alex said, "Go on and go."

Babs was torn. She really loved being with her friends and didn't like having her plans changed abruptly. Nevertheless, Alex was here and he was her fiancé. When her friends stopped to pick her up, Babs told them to go on.

Alex explained briefly why he had come back to the States unannounced, but a dark silence hung awkwardly between them. Normally good at conversing, Alex and Babs tried to make small talk, but neither seemed to know what to say. Babs began to wonder what married life would be like. Being with the young people was always fun; this wasn't. Furthermore, she really didn't like the mustache Alex now sported.

Alex felt crushed that Babs wasn't thrilled to see him. "What's wrong?" he asked, bewildered.

Babs replied, "Maybe when I'm old and gray, I'll tell you."

Doubts nibbled at Alex's self-esteem. Babs was extremely beautiful. He'd been gone for nineteen months. Perhaps she'd gotten interested in someone else. Maybe she'd begun wondering whether she should marry him. After all, on a missionary's salary of $60 a month, he certainly didn't have much to offer her.

The evening left both Alex and Babs feeling dejected.

Mrs. Babich told Alex how sorry she was as she took him to the guest room. Then she confronted her daughter with outrage. "How could you treat him like that?" she demanded. "He's pure gold and you'll never find another man as good as Alex."

Babs wasn't so sure. The next morning, she got up and went to work as usual. When Alex woke up later, he felt as though the engagement was about to end.

Sensing Alex's hurt, Babs's mother did her best to cheer him up. Then, in tears, she told Alex, "Don't stop and don't give up."

Downhearted but still in love with Babs, Alex bought her a dozen roses before taking the train to Passaic.

Babs was flabbergasted when she came home from work and found the roses. "It wasn't the roses," she says, still close to tears over fifty years later. "It was the note he sent with them. It said, 'With every petal of these roses, I wish to say that I love you.'

"When I read that, it hit me really hard: This man has a poetic, romantic side and he really does love me. I told my mother I'd made a dreadful mistake and through bitter tears asked her what to do.

"She said, 'I'd take a train to Passaic and make up if I were you.' So that's what I did."

When Alex found Babs at his door, it was his turn to be surprised.

And delighted.

Through a mixture of tears, hugs and kisses, they set their wedding date for February 23. That meant they had only a little over a month to complete their wedding plans!

Alex immediately sought the medical attention he needed to ward off the debilitating conditions that had sent him home. Proper medication, normal altitudes, familiar foods and a reduced schedule soon started him on the road to recovery.

Even in the midst of wedding plans and medical treatment, however, he did not forget his vision of reaching the Russian people by radio. "New Life" was still being broadcast because Alex had left prerecorded programs at HCJB, but it was now being aired weekly rather than daily. Even so, Alex knew that fresh programs would have to be made. Because of that, he began gathering recording equipment so he could produce new programs.

In addition, he traveled as a representative of RGA, encouraging others to pray for and give to the work of reaching the Soviet Union with the gospel. While visiting Russian churches, he also looked for choirs that could record hymns for use on the radio.

Alex and Babs were married on Sunday, February 23, 1947. Because the Russian Baptist Church was too small, the ceremony was held in the Conklin Methodist Church in South River.

Knowing that many unbelievers would attend the wedding, Alex and Babs asked the minister to begin the service with a gospel message and an invitation to accept Christ. When he finished, the wedding party entered.

Babs, wearing an elegant beaded satin gown and carrying a satin-covered Bible, started down the aisle on her father's arm. Halfway to the front, the organist stopped playing and Babs and her father stood silently while the minister asked, "Who gives this woman to wed this man?"

Her father answered, "Her mother and I do." Then he sat down with his wife, leaving Babs alone in the aisle. The soloist began singing, "Because you come to me . . ." as Alex walked from the front of the church to claim his bride so they could walk together to the altar to be united in marriage. Striking in its simplicity, the gesture brought tears to many eyes.

The women of the Russian church served a lavish reception at the Polish National Home. Then the newlyweds took a train to the Times Square Hotel for their wedding night. Having spent all of their time at the reception visiting instead of eating, they were famished. In addition, they were nervous and couldn't sleep. So, at 2:30 a.m., they ordered BLT sandwiches!

The next day Alex and Babs boarded a train for Miami. Two things made their honeymoon memorable: severe sunburn and a disquieting separation.

On their first Sunday as a married couple, they attended a large church in Miami. After the service, while Alex was visiting with many people, Babs went to the ladies' room. When she came back, the church was empty and she couldn't find Alex. Not knowing what else to do after she'd looked for him in the foyer, the auditorium and the halls, Babs decided to go back to the hotel.

Meanwhile, Alex realized Babs wasn't with him. He started searching for her in the auditorium and halls and then went outside. Desperate, Alex called the hospitals and the police station. Two hours later, a very distraught young husband went back to the hotel where he saw Babs walking in the hotel lobby.

Each exclaimed, "Where were you?" and then embraced, relieved at having lost only a few hours rather than each other.

After the honeymoon, the couple returned to New Jersey where they moved into four little rooms above Babs's parents.

Alex soon learned what a rich background his wife brought with her. Like clockwork every morning, her parents read Scripture together and sang hymns. After singing, they knelt, prayed and wept together.

"They were simple folks who left very little of material things but a great spiritual heritage of knowledge and love for the Lord and His people. Their faith was real. It became a great help and motivation for Babs and me," Alex remembers.

Once settled, Alex applied for a visa to the Soviet Union so he could see if his broadcasts were getting through. The request was denied.

Alex was disappointed but not surprised. Contact with his relatives had been very difficult ever since the mid-1930s when all direct correspondence and contact with the United States had been halted.

"We knew Stalin's regime had closed most of the Russian churches. A few of the larger churches were allowed to stay open so officials could say that they had religious freedom, but we knew most had been closed and many Christians had been and were being persecuted. There would have been no opportunity to do any evangelistic work, but I had hoped to find out if anyone was listening to 'New Life.' "

With only God's promise not to let His Word return void, Alex continued to produce programs and to pray that God's truth would reach the Russians via radio. He constantly did his best to keep the program fresh and lively by using good quality Russian music, drama and different speakers.

A.J. Overton's church in East Flat Rock, North Carolina, simplified the complicated process of cutting discs by giving Alex a Magnacord tape recorder so he could tape programs at his home. Without a soundproof studio, Alex had to wait until late at night to tape the programs so that outside noise would not interfere with the recording.

Bob Bowman and William J. Roberts, founders of Far East Broadcasting Company (FEBC), expanded Alex's short-wave outreach by asking for programs they could broadcast into Slavic countries. They did so without charge but at their own discretion.

During these years, Alex traveled extensively for RGA. A gifted communicator of the vision and challenges of reaching Russians with the gospel, he was constantly in demand as a speaker for missionary conferences.

Alex's schedule for 1948 took him throughout the western United States and Canada. To avoid a prolonged separation, Babs resigned from her job and went along, leaving home, friends, job and church.

While in Montana, she became so sick she went to a doctor. He told her, "It's just the high altitude. This often happens to young girls." At Calgary, she also felt so sick that she sought a doctor. Again she was told it was just the altitude.

When they got home months later, Babs went to her family doctor. He ended the mystery by telling her, "You're pregnant."

David was born on October 30, 1948. Babs especially enjoyed caring for her little son, often singing hymns and gospel songs or quoting Scripture as she held and nursed him.

Alex felt torn by his new responsibilities. He was excited about being a father and wanted to be involved in David's life but felt he had to honor his vows to put Christ first. Babs agreed and Alex continued traveling in itinerant ministry and producing "New Life."

Three and a half years had passed since he had made his first broadcast. Many Russian immigrants in South America, Australia, Finland, Canada and the United States wrote to say how much they benefitted from the broadcasts, but an occasional lone postcard was the only hint Alex had that anyone was listening in the Soviet Union.

As he had done every year since the end of the war, Alex again applied for a visa to visit the USSR, thinking that if he could actually go there, he might be able to get some idea if the time, energy and resources he devoted to making the programs were worth it. Once again, his request was rejected. Once again, no reason was given.

Alex knew other Americans were allowed to travel to the Soviet Union. After many refusals, he finally concluded that his proficiency in Russian made him a threat. Because other Americans spoke no Russian, they would understand only what the government agents told them, making them easy prey for communist propaganda. Alex, on the other hand, knew Russian fluently and could understand not only what was said but also what was implied. A repressive regime feared he would learn too much!

Alex could do nothing but pray in his efforts to get his visa approved. God seemed to give only one answer: *Trust Me. My calendar is different from yours and My ways are different than yours. Live and work one day at a time.*

Only goodness meeting evil and not infected by it,
conquers evil.

—Leo Tolstoy, *What I Believe*, 1882

CHAPTER 8

"SINCE WE COULDN'T GO TO RUSSIA . . ."
1949-1953: Europe

IN THE WAKE OF World War II, tensions and hostilities continued to simmer as people tried to make sense out of all the suffering.

Early in the war, Hitler's troops took hundreds of thousands of Russian citizens as prisoners of war to work as slave laborers on farms and in factories throughout Europe. When Germany lost the war, the USSR demanded that they be returned. The Russians, however, refused to go back to the Soviet Union and the Western powers insisted that the people be granted freedom to settle wherever they chose.

While their fate was being decided, the Russians were placed in large camps of 1,500 to 10,000 people each where they became known as displaced persons (DPs).

The DPs lived day to day in cramped, uncomfortable conditions with no place to go, no work to do and no idea what their future held. Feeling like pawns in a slippery game of political chess, some DPs threw themselves in front of the wheels of Allied tanks and trucks or jumped off bridges with babies tied to their bodies to demonstrate that they would rather die than be sent back to the Soviet Union.

Their clear, adamant stand made negotiators wonder about the West's precarious wartime alliance with the USSR and added new ice to the rapidly chilling Cold War.

Peter Deyneka preached in some of the DP camps in 1948. Soon, he dreamed of sending a team to minister to the refugees, a vision he shared with his friends Torrey Johnson and Bob Cook, co-founders of a dynamic new organization known as Youth For Christ (YFC).

At the YFC Conference at Winona Lake, Indiana, that July, Deyneka prayed for the DPs during an all-night session of prayer and fasting. Before the conference ended, YFC decided to send a team to the camps to preach the gospel and take much-needed supplies. Deyneka approached Alex, who was working for RGA, and said, "Alex, we want you to go."

Alex hated to leave his family. But the need was great, so in the spring of 1949, amidst many tears, Alex hugged his little family to himself and left for Europe on the *Queen Mary*.

It was not an easy assignment. The communists had demonstrated their penchant for world revolution and domination in June 1948 when they blockaded Berlin to keep food, fuel and other necessities from the people. The United States Air Force responded by airlifting supplies in a massive operation known as the Berlin Airlift. As they began their own mission of mercy, Alex and the other men on the team immediately noticed that the planes were still flying over East Germany every ninety seconds to deliver supplies to Berlin.

The team first stopped at the DP camp in Naples, Italy. Then they drove their 1948 wood-paneled brown Chevrolet station wagon which had been donated by Mrs. Kerr of the Kerr Canning Company, to the next camp. The wagon, always packed with supplies, faithfully took them to hundreds of camps scattered throughout Italy, Germany, Belgium and France.

Alex recalls, "Whenever we came into a camp, nearly everyone stopped what they were doing to come to our gospel service. They were in a helpless, hopeless situation where they were strangers in strange lands with a foreign language and culture. Our coming was something to break the monotony of the day.

"We became a testimony of Christian concern for both their physical needs and their spiritual needs, as we always used the supplies we brought to demonstrate the love of Christ. We never went with empty hands but instead took something to give to those in need, especially the boys and girls and the elderly.

"We came as people who spoke their language and understood their plight, bringing whatever we could to ease their suffering and give them hope.

"Tears flowed freely in every service. They realized there was no other deliverance than what God could give and many thousands came to know Christ as personal Savior.

"In one camp of 1,500, everyone accepted Christ. We never had enough Bibles or gospel literature to satisfy them. They were so hungry to hear the Word of God they would stand for hours."

Despite the warm reception by the DPs, the team was continually stopped by customs officials, who detained them for hours by interrogating them and searching through everything in the station wagon. As they waited, Alex noticed that priests in clerical garb were allowed to go through immediately.

Frustrated by the time-wasting delays, Alex says, "At that time, there were disposable collars, so I decided to get one. Then I took one of the black skirts from the piles of clothes we were taking to the refugees, put the collar on backwards, tucked the skirt under the collar, bloused it out a little and put my jacket on.

"The next time I went through customs, the official bowed to me and waved me through. I had to bite my lip to keep from laughing. No one had ever bowed to me before! After that, as long as I wore my 'ministerial outfit,' I had no trouble."

Although Alex's team physically delivered the supplies, they recognized that they were part of a much larger team. "We couldn't have done it without the help of Christians in the United States," Alex says.

"They gave money and supplies so we could give to the people.

"As I worked with the people in the camps, I saw that God uses even the problems and foolishness of man for His glory. When things are easy, our noses point to the ground, but when we're in agony on our backs, we suddenly start looking heavenward for our help.

"The Lord used the problems and persecution to awaken the people's consciences so they could see that help was not of man but only of God. God used their tears and the agony of being separated from their homeland and families to help them find the One who 'sticks closer than a brother' (Proverbs 18:24, NIV) and the One who is our Helper in the time of need."

In the last three months of the tour, the team held rallies in England, Scotland and Wales where some of the Russian refugees had begun to settle. Alex still longed to visit the land of his birth so he could share Christ with those cut off from the rest of the world by Stalin's repressive policies. Nevertheless, he was grateful for this opportunity to minister to so many of those who spoke his native tongue, especially since they seemed so appreciative of the team's efforts.

"It became apparent to me that since we couldn't go to Russia, God had used World War II to bring the Russian people to us," Alex recalls. "Those days were filled with the assurance that we were on the right path as far as knowing and doing the will of God."

◊ ◊ ◊ ◊ ◊ ◊ ◊ ◊

Alex returned home in December 1949. It was a tearful reunion. Having been in Europe for nine months, Alex was overjoyed to see his family. But he was also taken aback: "My one-year-old son didn't recognize me because I'd been gone so long. I'd missed his first words, his first steps and his first birthday.

"I started to think deeply into my life, because we cannot be more concerned for those in the outside world than we are for those closest at home. I realized that I had tremendous responsibility to my own family and saw that it was possible to be so caught up in the work of reaching others that we neglect those closest to us."

From then on, Alex did his best to limit his speaking engagements to those geographically nearer home. He had been home for only a few months, however, when Peter Deyneka asked him to return to HCJB to head the Russian Department and assist in the studios while workers went on furlough.

Alex felt torn. He wanted to help, but he hated being separated from his family again. On the other hand, he and Babs had promised to put God first. Feeling that he had an obligation to go because he was on the staff of the Slavic Gospel Association (formerly RGA), Alex left in February 1950.

While at HCJB, Alex focused his attention almost entirely on radio and this time had no problems with Quito's altitude.

When the furloughed workers returned, Alex began his trip home. On the way, he flew to Venezuela where he held meetings, baptized those who had come to the Lord through the Russian programs on HCJB and helped start mission stations in Valencia, Caracas, Marakai and Maracaibo. Alex spoke at YFC rallies in Trinidad, Jamaica and Cuba. The fact that he was Russian drew large crowds, because people automatically assumed that all Russians were communists, making them curious to hear what he would say.

Babs and two-year-old David met him in Cuba. Their reunion was a joyous time of reaffirmation of their love for one another and of their commitment to serve Christ wherever and whenever He called, regardless of culture, language or place.

Once Alex returned home, however, a few close friends and Babs's parents told him how lonely Babs was while he was gone.

"Babs never presented anything but a happy face to me even when I was leaving," Alex says. "I had to learn from others that her pillow was often wet with tears when I was gone."

Alex agonized over the situation. He and Babs had pledged to always put God first when they'd agreed to get married. Called to be a missionary to the Russian people, Alex had seen God work mightily as he traveled around the world. If he stopped traveling, would he be reneging on his commitment to the Lord? Yet First Timothy 5:8 gave another priority: "But if any provide not for his own, and specially for those of his own house, he hath denied the faith, and is worse than an infidel."

What was involved in "providing for his own"? Food and shelter, yes, but what about affection and companionship? If Babs were so lonely she was crying herself to sleep, something was wrong. And David . . . he didn't want David to grow up without a father.

Alex prayed earnestly for the Lord's leading. A heavy schedule of traveling for Slavic Gospel Association (SGA) and YFC loomed ahead with meetings and rallies criss-crossing the United States and Canada. As he looked at the itinerary, he decided to take Babs and David along.

During the summer, they lived in the SGA offices on Kedzie Boulevard in Chicago and ministered among the many Russians of German ancestry who had been pushed out of Russia and now lived in Wisconsin, North Dakota and Illinois.

Later, his schedule called for extensive travel in Canada holding meetings with Grady Wilson of the Billy Graham Evangelistic Association. Alex and Babs decided it would be better if she and David stayed in Chicago at the Missions House where she would not have to travel every day and could work in the SGA office. Chicago's location allowed Alex to come home more often to spend time with his family.

Missionary conferences, deputation work and Saturday night YFC rallies in Canada and the Midwest

filled their days until early February 1952. Then Alex
and Babs returned to New Jersey to surround themselves with family and friends as they awaited the birth
of their second child. Diane Ruth, whom they immediately called by the Russian equivalent, Deena, was
born on February 18, 1952.

Later that year, as he saw how quickly Alex's engagement calendar filled up and how well people responded when Alex spoke, Peter Deyneka tried to
persuade Alex to give up his Russian-speaking ministries and work full-time as an SGA field representative to English-speaking churches.

"As I thought and prayed about the offer, I realized
that God had given me a gift with the Russian language," Alex remembers. "Young people coming to
America learned English easily, but some of their parents would never learn enough English in their lifetimes
to really understand spiritual truths. I felt God wanted
me to work directly with the Slavic people rather than
devote myself completely to traveling and raising funds."

Explaining this to Deyneka, however, was not easy.
Deyneka had been the one who had challenged Alex to
go into full-time missionary service. He had served as
Alex's mentor and boss. And Deyneka, of course,
hadn't acquired the nickname of "Peter Dynamite"
without earning it!

Following through on his decision to leave SGA
meant leaving a visible and profitable ministry for an
obscure and unknown future.

Through the months of transition, Alex continued broadcasting over HCJB and holding meetings. But he also continued working directly with Russian immigrants.

Early in 1953, the South River Russian Baptist Church asked Alex to serve as their pastor. In that role, he could work with Russian young people, who were eager to be Americans, and with their parents, who clung to Russian ways, without having to leave his family constantly. Seeing the opportunity as God's way of weaving the strands of his life together, Alex accepted their call and left SGA.

Alex's strong desire was to preach to those living in his motherland. For now, however, he again focused on ministering to the Russian people the Lord brought to him.

Although he had no idea what his future held, Alex knew that, for now, his family needed more of his time and he needed to remain involved with the Russian community. "After all," he says, "we're no more effective among far and distant people than among people in our own Jerusalem."

The duties of home are discipline for the ministries of heaven.

—Anonymous

CHAPTER 9

HEART FOR HOME
1953-1966: New Jersey

ALEX'S DECISION USHERED IN profound changes. Instead of traveling from city to city as the missionary speaker, he became responsible for the day-to-day nitty-gritty shepherding of a local church, a position he took with some trepidation since he had no experience in such a role.

Having changed course in order to have more time with his family, he determined that no matter what else he needed to do, he would give Babs the love and support she needed and his children the childhood he never had. That in no way supplanted his commitment to the Lord or the ministries to which God called him, however. "Full surrender" meant full surrender . . . not for a few years, but for a lifetime. Alex entered this new era of his life committed to excellence in ministry for his family, his church and his native land.

In his initial meeting with the church board in February 1953, they asked, "What do you expect as a salary?"

Alex answered, "Our policy from day one has been to never put a dollar sign on our ministry. If we have been called of the Lord to do a certain job, we haven't asked what we would receive. Instead, we've believed God would supply our needs."

His policy was tested the very first month when he was given only $40.

"It was hardly enough to pay our rent to Babs's parents. But the Lord put His seal of approval on our ministry by having a local grocer call to say there was a package there for us. When I arrived at the store, I found three bushel baskets filled with food, including some little things for the home. Our wants as well as our needs were provided, and all we could say was, 'How like the Lord!' "

Just two months after the church in South River called Alex to be their pastor, the Emmanuel Baptist Church in Manville asked him to also serve as their interim pastor.

"I came as they were starting their building program," Alex recalls. "It was a very warm and supportive church filled with much love and fellowship."

As both churches grew, Alex felt that South River also needed to build a larger facility. Some of the older members thought that was foolish. One man said, "If some older one taught me, I would listen, but when a *molokosos* (little child; one who feeds on the breast) tries to tell me something . . . ."

Alex understood the tradition out of which the words came, and wept. He didn't want to offend those who were older; he simply felt the church needed to take advantage of the opportunities around them. Feeling strongly that God had led him into the pastorate and that God was leading them to build, Alex persisted. But, wise beyond his years, he opted to simply absorb the man's comments rather than defend himself, believing that "love covers a multitude of sins."

Despite the opposition, the South River congregation built a beautiful place of worship. Years later, Alex said, "The man who was the biggest opponent became the closest of friends and a strong supporter, but it took a lot of patience and and prayer to win him over."

Babs says, "The Lord gave Alex a lot of grace and love. I would have quit because it would have bothered me to have someone against me."

Alex just shrugs his shoulders and says, "My feeling is that a servant is no greater than his Master. What right do I have to expect more than the Lord received? I was happy to be identified with the Lord, even in this kind of a situation, to prove that the love within us is greater than any power which can conquer us from the outside."

Eager to grow, the Manville church began an annual city-wide outreach program which included teams from Practical Bible Training School in Johnson City, New

York. The students gained valuable experience in cross-cultural ministry as they worked among the ethnically diverse groups in Manville. People responded well to the young people because they represented so many different backgrounds that they called their choir the "League of Many Nations." Their concerts always drew enthusiastic crowds.

Concern for children led to Bible clubs, after-school ministries and a Sunday school program which overflowed into three old buses which were transformed into classrooms.

During these years when income was meager, Alex received other offers to pastor larger churches or to work for companies where he could make more money. Without exception, he refused, seeing the South River and Manville churches as those to which God had called him.

Both churches were bilingual. Both needed leadership. Alex divided his time between them. Knowing criticism would bother Babs, Alex never told her of difficulties so she could always greet people with a warm smile.

Babs says, "Of course, Alex did a lot of smiling too. And he helped me grow a lot. I never knew whom he would bring home, but he always told me not to worry: 'Whatever you have, share. It doesn't need to be fancy; it's the fellowship that's important.' "

The simple concept of sharing rather than entertaining took the burden out of preparing for guests, as did Alex's willingness to pitch in and help. Because Alex and Babs both loved people, they wove a strong, supportive web for those within their care, extending warm hospitality to anyone who needed food, clothing or a place to stay.

While pastoring the two churches, Alex also began an English broadcast on radio station WCTC in New Brunswick, NJ, entitled, "Songs of Praises." He recorded the program after Sunday dinner and then rushed the tape to the radio station. It became a family tradition to listen after Sunday night church.

"He made it interesting by including music as well as preaching," his daughter, Dawn, says, "He kept it moving so people wanted to keep listening and lots of non-Christians did. It was really short, about ten minutes, I think."

Relevant and lively, the program became a springboard from which people asked Alex for help with their problems or spiritual needs wherever he went, including the supermarket and the post office.

Alex also fostered intense involvement in world missions by building on what the churches were already doing. The Manville Church had launched Mary Selody into the ministry on August 3, 1933 so she could found an orphanage in Carpathia, Russia. Forced to flee from Russia to Hungary to Germany during World War II, she began working in DP camps.

Alex had an understanding of the great needs around the world and actively encouraged his members to support their missionaries in practical ways, such as preparing relief packages of clothing for those in Russia and the DP camps. His enthusiasm was so contagious that many young people chose to go to Bible colleges to prepare for ministries around the world. Alex says, "It wasn't spectacular but it was steady, and it constantly encouraged us to keep our spirits up and our faith strong."

Attending the RUEBU Conventions in Ashford, Connecticut, each summer also expanded the churches' vision for a needy world and helped them build relationships with many of the leaders, including Dr. Kmeta and Dr. Ivan V. Neprash, founder of the Russian Missionary Service (RMS).

On April 13, 1957, Dr. Neprash died suddenly after suffering a heart attack on his way home from speaking at New York City's Calvary Baptist Church. Dr. Neprash had structured RMS from its inception to partner with national Christians to establish indigenous churches using national workers who knew the language, culture, problems and needs of the people. The nationals in Poland, Europe, Canada and South America were more economical to support and more readily trusted than outsiders but had no way to raise the finances they needed by themselves. Dr. Neprash's untimely death left RMS without a head, causing public confidence and financial backing to nose-dive.

After a few months, some who had supported RMS approached Mrs. Neprash saying, "Just because a person dies doesn't mean his work should die with him."

Mrs. Neprash agreed and asked RUEBU to take RMS under its umbrella. The Union agreed to do so, but since it already had its own missionaries, it could not do much to help the floundering RMS ministries. In an effort to salvage the situation, RUEBU asked Alex to serve as the Executive Director of RMS.

Believing wholeheartedly in the concept of nationals reaching nationals and recognizing their need for a stateside spokesman, Alex asked Babs and the churches to pray about the situation. Everyone came to the same conclusion: Alex should accept the position.

Alex says, "Heading an organization such as RMS was something I had never done before. I would have preferred mundane work, but I was willing to take leadership if that was what was needed."

Because the outreach of RMS included those who were Ukrainian and Polish as well as those who were Russian, Alex asked that the organization's name be changed to Slavic Missionary Service (SMS). His appointment as executive secretary of the newly organized SMS was announced in January 1958, and he set up offices in two rooms at the South River church.

It was a troubled time. SMS had no money, not even for postage stamps. Alex had only a list of donors, some faithful volunteers and his own ingenuity to get the organization going again. He took speaking engagements when he could fit them into his schedule, but with primary responsibilities for two churches and his family, Alex was limited in the time he could devote to traveling. Nevertheless, little by little, momentum began to pick up, and SMS not only survived, but once again began to thrive.

Later that year, friend and parishioner Ben Lawson talked Alex into buying a half-acre property that Ben had acquired as partial payment for some cows and horses he'd sold.

Certain that Alex should have the land because it was located midway between the churches in South River and Manville, Ben offered to co-sign so Alex could get a small loan. Although Alex hated to borrow money, he realized that the land was an outstanding investment when a neighbor offered Ben three times the amount he was asking from Alex.

When Alex went to price lumber, the Middlebush Lumber Yard gave him all the lumber he needed on a handshake and then offered Babs a job as a secretary. Both Alex and Babs saw this as the clear provision of the Lord, and Alex began building a house for his growing family.

"When I was home, I nailed at least one board each day, often in a suit coat, white shirt and tie. Before long, I became known as the 'Gentleman Laborer,' " he remembers.

By the time their third child, Dawn Marie, was born on August 23, 1960, Alex had completed a lovely white frame house with a brick front. It featured a long living room with a brick wall, complete with a fireplace, a balcony and a cathedral-style ceiling. In memory of the land of his birth, Alex planted several white birch trees near the house.

Having a place of their own was like a dream come true for the little family that had lived above the Babiches for over ten years. David and Deena were able to have separate bedrooms and everyone enjoyed the family room and backyard.

On October 16, 1960, "New Life" also found a new home when Trans World Radio began broadcasting from Monte Carlo, Monaco.

Founded in 1952 in Tangier, Morocco, by Alex's college friend, Dr. Paul Freed, TWR was forced off the air in 1959 when newly independent Morocco opted to nationalize all radio stations. Through a series of miracles, Freed was able to replace the Tangier station with a fabulous facility in Monte Carlo which the Germans had erected during WWII. Their plan was to use it to broadcast Nazi propaganda, but the war ended before they were able to install equipment. Now it would be used to broadcast the gospel into the Iron Curtain countries.

Freed summarizes it this way: "The devil outdid himself that time. He closed us up with 10,000 watts in Tangier. But God opened us up with 100,000 watts in Monte Carlo, a thousand miles closer to Moscow!"[1]

Those interested in getting through the Iron Curtain with the gospel immediately saw this as an exciting opportunity to expand shortwave coverage in the Soviet Union.

Alex's brother, Nick, who had beamed Russian programs into the satellite countries when he started working as TWR's director of Russian broadcasting on the Voice of Tangier in the late 1950s, helped orchestrate the new effort.

Alex was allowed a small peek into how short-wave Christian broadcasting was being received in the Soviet Union when he secured permission for the South River church to host Michael Zhidkov, the first Russian student allowed to study in the West. Michael's father, Jacob, had served as one of the leaders of the Russian Baptist movement during Stalin's regime, and Alex had gotten acquainted with him through RUEBU. Wanting Michael to visit the South River church while he studied at McMaster University in Hamilton, Ontario, Alex petitioned his congressman to allow the visit.

Michael told the congregation, "I'm glad to be here in your land of freedom. Looking into your faces, however, I don't know which is worse: your freedom or our lack of it.

"I feel that our lack of freedom may be better because it purges and cleanses and we have no wishy-washyness, while your overabundance of freedom leads to license to sin and compromise. In Russia there are no Sunday-morning Christians. The cost is too high to be nominal. It's either total commitment or nothing at all."

While visiting, Michael took Alex aside to tell him that Christians with shortwave radios really appreciated the Russian broadcasts. It was a welcome word of encouragement to the man who had been broadcasting for fifteen years.

Michael's visit came during the ambivalent years of Nikita Khrushchev, head of the Communist Party after Stalin's death in March 1953. Having severely condemned Stalin for ruthlessness and brutality in a landmark de-Stalinization speech in February of 1956, Khrushchev provided some respite in the '50s from the severe repressions and persecution experienced under Stalin in the '30s and '40s. His liberalization of some of Stalin's most stringent policies led to the release of many political prisoners and to a wave of revival and church growth.

The relaxation was short-lived, however. Many church leaders were arrested in 1957 and an all-out attack on Christians was launched in 1959. Krushchev, once concerned about convincing the world that Soviet citizens enjoyed religious freedom, now boasted that religion would be relegated to museums and Christians obliterated by 1980.[2]

Despite Khrushchev's yo-yo policies and threats of world domination, Alex continued to prepare and send programs to HCJB, FEBC and TWR. He also carried out the myriad of duties involved in pastoring two churches, heading SMS and caring for his family. Because the Manville church was expanding rapidly and SMS demanded many hours, the workload finally forced Alex to resign from the South River church in 1960.

During these days of great pressure and sparse income, Alex answered a knock on his door. The gentlemen standing there identified themselves as CIA agents and said, "Your name has been given to us with the highest recommendation that you work for the CIA because of your background and knowledge of Russia."

Flabbergasted, Alex replied, "I feel honored to be asked to do this, but I feel I can serve my country best by serving God and giving my life to work among the Slavic people."

Alex's understanding of that call extended beyond evangelism and preaching to actively meeting people's needs. Adopting eleven-year-old Marion Clingenpeel while Dawn was still an infant showed the priority he placed on living out one's profession of Christianity.

Marion's mother had died from leukemia when Marion was only two. Because her father, George, had to work, he feared he would have to send Marion to an orphanage. Alex and Babs offered to adopt Marion and care for all her needs, including a college education, if George would sign papers so she would be legally theirs if he died. George readily ageed, saying, "I didn't think there were those kinds of people left in the world."

Filled with motherly instincts, Marion helped care for Dawn. Twelve-year-old David did not see Marion's good qualities, however. To him, she was a competitor, and he made no secret of his animosity toward her saying, "She's got relatives," he complained. "Why can't they care for her?"

David's rejection of Marion troubled Alex and Babs. They prayed about it and did their best to help David and Marion work out their differences, but the impasse continued. Alex was feeling especially discouraged about the situation one evening. As he started to enter the house, he heard David and Marion shouting at each other. When he investigated, he found them engaged in an all-out pillow fight.

Instead of rushing in to stop them, Alex cried, "Praise the Lord!" because he saw the fight as a breathrough in David's ability to accept Marion as a sister.

He was right. The fight cleared the air so David and Marion could learn to get along as siblings.

The next year, the Leonovich home opened its doors to welcome Alex's sister, Betty, her husband, Paul Semenchuk, and their boys. After serving as missionaries to the DPs in Europe, the Semenchuks joined the staff of SMS as Field Representatives in 1959. Because most of their assignments were in the south, they had plans to move to Florida when Paul and the boys came down with mumps. Paul's case was so severe that his doctor forbade him to move.

The Semenchuks found a missionary cottage in Ventnor, New Jersey, where they stayed for a year. At the end of that time, however, they were not able to find another place they could afford. Alex offered to let them move into their newly finished home. Thinking it would be for just a few weeks or months, the families agreed.

Betty says, "We stayed in the lower level of the house, but we all lived as one family. One week Babs cooked; the next I did. We had one kitty; all of us donated to buy the food. Both Babs and I worked, so Al and Paul took turns taking care of the kids when they weren't traveling for SMS.

"We were there for two-and-a-half years and there was no friction at all. The seven kids got along so well that we wish we could do it again."

In March 1964, Paul and Betty and their sons, Tim, Dan and Jeff, left for Monte-Carlo to assist brother Nick with the Russian programming at TWR.

The Semenchuks and Marion stayed longer than most, but represented only a few of the many who had their needs met in the Leonovich home. "It was always like Grand Central Station at our house. We had people in all the time," Babs says.

Dawn adds, "The different people who joined us for Sunday dinners and suppers broadened our perspective on life."

David remembers Saturday fishing trips, ball games and an assortment of practical jokes, some of which he played on his father, such as stuffing his pants with books before being spanked or fastening an old shoe to his father's fishing line. "Overall, he did well with jokes so long as someone wasn't being hurt," is David's assessment.

The girls remember their father as the one who braided their hair for school because their mother was working. Deena says, "We just couldn't make ends meet on what the churches paid Dad, so Mom worked. Dad often shopped for groceries, cooked and washed dishes. He was the one who was here when we came home from school. And if we needed anything mended, we took it to him because he could mend it so you could hardly see it."

"Overall, he was encouraging and optimistic," Deena says about her dad. "He always seemed to know the right word to say to make us feel better."

Alex had given up extensive traveling to devote more time to his family, but he never lost his enthusiasm for reaching the Slavic peoples of the world.

The only significance of life consists in helping to establish the kingdom of God; and this can be done only by means of the acknowledgment and profession of the truth by every one of us.

—Leo Tolstoy,
The Kingdom of God, 1893

CHAPTER 10

THE BOX THAT CREATED QUESTIONS
1941-1965: Leningrad, Moscow, Kharkov, Kiev, Minsk, Warsaw

OVER THE YEARS ALEX'S desire to return to his homeland to preach the gospel throbbed stronger and stronger. "I lived in hope of being able to reach my people not only by radio but by standing on the soil of my birth," Alex says. "It was a burning passion and I looked for any avenue where my dream could become a reality."

As Alex began to participate in RUEBU activities, he discovered a kindred spirit in the organization's president, Dr. Ivan Kmeta. Both men shared a deep inner drive to revisit their homeland and preach the gospel there. Each year they applied for visas. Each year they were denied. Yet, instead of giving up, both men simply became more determined.

As they waited, Alex and Dr. Kmeta monitored the political and religious pulse of the USSR, noting that the forced closure of many churches, the convoluted regulations for registration and the ban prohibiting young people under eighteen from attending services were driving wedges between believers.

"We ought to obey God rather than men" (Acts 5:29) became the rallying cry for increasing numbers of Pentecostals and Baptists who felt forced to form unregistered groups while registered churches felt compelled to obey the scriptural injunction in Romans 13:1 "Let every soul be subject unto the higher powers. For there is no power but of God: the powers that be are ordained of God."

Both sides were torn over the issues, especially as those in unregistered groups were fined, arrested and imprisoned with increasing frequency.

The government attacks galvanized believers into a movement for reform. In January 1963, a group appealed to the American Embassy in Moscow for help in emigrating because of religious persecution. Although their request was denied, their plight drew protests from the West. Khrushchev, however, continued to escalate his antireligious campaign.

October 1964 brought abrupt changes when Khruschev was suddenly ousted from power by his Politburo colleagues. Leonid Brezhnev and his regime softened the government's stance, releasing some of those who had been imprisoned and downsizing open persecution.

When Dr. Kmeta invited Russian representatives to attend the 1965 RUEBU Conference in Ashford, Connecticut, Soviet authorities surprised the churches by agreeing to let four pastors from registered churches attend.

Alex and Dr. Kmeta detected a guarded wariness when the Russian pastors arrived in July. They seemed to weigh each word and evaluate each action with questions such as: *Why were we allowed to come? Are we being used for propaganda purposes? Who's watching us so they can report us? What will happen to us—and to our churches—when we return to the Soviet Union?*

The pastors showed signs of long-term intimidation in trying to balance the burden of caring for their congregations in the face of criticism from those who pictured them as compromisers because they tried to cooperate with the government. It was as if they were tightrope walkers on ropes where the tensions kept changing and safety nets had been removed.

Although their relationships were somewhat strained, Alex found his interest in visiting Russia soar. "Meeting with the brethren in July just rekindled my desire to go to encourage the Church and to find out what effect 'New Life' was having."

Before they left, the visiting pastors promised to invite Alex and Dr. Kmeta to come to the Soviet Union on a reciprocal visit, an accepted courtesy within Russian culture.

Hoping the government would honor such an invitation, Dr. Kmeta and Alex again applied for visas. This time, they received official invitations for a fall visit.

"We immediately filled out the detailed questionnaires and tried to find out the limitations of what we would and wouldn't be able to do," Alex says. "Then we began preparing ourselves spiritually and emotionally to be used by God. Both Dr. Kmeta and I wanted to be very careful lest any mistake on our part would close doors in the future."

The trip sparked great controversy. Colleagues criticized them for going, saying, "You must have sold out to the government; the real Church is underground."

Alex recalls, "Some wouldn't come right out and call us 'red,' but intimated that we were 'pink.' "

With Western colleagues questioning him for being too soft on communism and the Soviets calling him a traitor, it was no wonder Alex's heart clattered like a freight train as he stood in line at the Leningrad Airport. Having the eyes and ears of Intourist and KGB agents scrutinize every move was unnerving. Alex quickly gained a new appreciation for the fear and uncertainty which constantly dogged his Russian brothers and sisters.

Because reports in the West pictured the registered churches as compromised and weak, Alex could not have been more surprised at the commitment and vitality he witnessed when he walked into the Leningrad Baptist Church. Forty men on their knees praying both before and during the three-hour service each Sunday and 1,800 enthusiastic worshipers jammed into a building designed to hold 450 challenged all preconceived American stereotypes. When Alex also learned that nearly all of the believers listened to his broadcasts to sustain them in an atheistic society, he felt weak-kneed before the Sovereign God who was quietly at work behind the scenes.

Alex's experiences at the Leningrad Baptist Church were only the first of many amazing events on his long-awaited trip back to his motherland.

After the service, in an effort to escape the ever-present eyes and ears of the KGB, Pastor Kerukhantsev invited Alex and Dr. Kmeta to a restaurant for dinner. As they walked to the restaurant, the pastor said, "I just want you to know how effective radio really is.

"One night there was a knock at my door. When I answered the door, I became very frightened because the man who was standing there was Andrey Tupolev."

Tupolev had designed the world's first supersonic passenger plane. Arrested by Soviet authorities so they could force him to build military aircraft during World War II, he had become so well-known that he could not go anywhere without four or five bodyguards.

"Tupolev saw how scared I looked and said, 'Everything's all right, but I just have to speak with you.'

"Then he told his bodyguards he had some matters he wished to discuss with me privately and asked them to wait outside.

"I invited him in. After I shut the door, he pointed to the shortwave radio standing in the corner and said, 'That box has created more questions in my mind than it's been able to answer. I'm a regular listener to Trans World Radio and I've been trying to get answers to some of the questions that the programs like "New Life" have brought to my mind. No one has been able to give me answers, but some people told me to come to you.'

"We talked for nearly three hours and I had the joy of leading him to the Lord."

When Alex and Dr. Kmeta left Leningrad, they traveled to Moscow, where they preached to 2,500 people in the Sunday morning service in a church designed to hold 600. Again, people arrived three hours early and crowded together, standing on every square inch, including the stairs. Again, a great gasp went up when "Brothers Kmeta and Leonovich" were introduced. Again, vitality and spiritual hunger permeated the congregation, and leaders begged parishioners attending morning services to stay home for the rest of the week's services.

To accommodate those wishing to worship, additional services were held on Tuesdays, Thursdays and Saturdays. The church was also packed for those services, often lasting for two-and-a-half to four hours.

From Moscow, Alex and Dr. Kmeta boarded a train to go to Kharkov. Officials planning their itinerary, however, had never told the Kharkov pastor, Danel Shapoval. Instead, in an effort to catch Shapoval off guard, KGB agents approached him while the Americans were en route and asked, "Why are Kmeta and Leonovich coming?"

Although surprised, Shapoval answered tactfully, "Perhaps they are coming to see our city and culture."

Once alerted that Alex and Dr. Kmeta were on their way to Kharkov, however, the pastor told his Sunday congregations, "We anticipate having guests from America tomorrow."

By 2 p.m. on Monday, the church was full. A twenty-eight voice male choir from the coal mining region of Dunbas which had traveled all night to sing at the service, gave Alex goose bumps. "Their rich harmony reverberated so much I worried that the roof would not be able to contain the sound."

The service started at 6 p.m. and lasted until 10 p.m. When the benediction was pronounced, the crowd swarmed around Dr. Kmeta and Alex to shake their hands and hug them.

Suddenly, loud voices from the rear of the auditorium began saying, "Dear Lord, You see how the devil is trying to destroy our faith."

Realizing that demonstrators from the unregistered churches were trying to instigate trouble so that they would be arrested in front of the Westerners, Shapoval quickly led the congregation in singing, "I Need Thee Every Hour," to drown out the dissent.

Alex and Dr. Kmeta were quickly ushered to a rear exit to return to their hotel. Several dissidents pushed their way through the crowd and shouted that they wanted the men to be aware of their persecution. Then they attempted to stuff papers about their mistreatment into Alex's and Dr. Kmeta's pockets.

The two men knew they could not accept the literature and climbed into the waiting Intourist taxi. The demonstrators responded by grabbing hold of the car to stop it by brute force and then started singing loudly.

Alex says, "They were hoping the police would arrest them so we would see how oppressed they were. They called themselves 'holier people,' but, in this case, they simply had enthusiasm and zeal without knowledge. I feel they were misinformed in trying to provoke trouble. Fortunately, the police didn't come and everything died down on its own."

The incident highlighted the tension which was growing between believers. Church closures, an inability to obtain licenses for new churches, concerns about compromise and the ban on bringing children to church had driven many to join unregistered churches despite the risk of discrimination, arrest and imprisonment.

Those in registered churches hated the restrictions which prevented them from bringing their children to services but felt that disobeying the law blackened their witness and gave the authorities an excuse for taking their children from them and closing all churches. They decided it was better to work within the law and do all they could to teach their children at home.

Alex understood the dilemma and was often asked what he would have done. "Sometimes we must accept the lesser of two evils," he responded. "Scripture tells us to 'Be wise as serpents and harmless as doves' (Matthew 10:16). The registered church chose to obey the government and trust God to work out the details, which gave them the opportunity to worship publicly and eventually led to our being able to visit to encourage the believers. But, to be honest, we were amazed by the spirit and energy of both sides."

God was at work in both movements, but it was sometimes difficult for those squeezed by pressure and persecution to see that. Alex tried to help them see the bigger picture by saying, "What the enemy couldn't accomplish through persecution, you're allowing to happen by fighting among yourselves. If we're going to be in heaven together, we need to learn how to live and work together here on earth. After all, there aren't going to be special streets for different groups in heaven."

When Dr. Kmeta and Alex left Kharkov, they traveled to Kiev where they again experienced overcrowding, gasps of recognition and tears of joy.

In Kiev, they were invited to a special tea in their honor at the Yamaskaya Church. Associate pastor Matvey Melnik took Alex aside and pointed out a man in a gray suit who was sitting in a corner with his back to them. "Alex," he said. "That man was once the head KGB man for this area. We were afraid of his shadow until he came to know the Lord through Nick's broadcast. Now, he who once persecuted the church is himself being persecuted."

Alex quickly made his way to the man who turned around just as Alex got there. As the men stood, Alex said, "Dear brother, I just heard how you came to the Lord."

The two men immediately embraced each other and wept. Alex said, "I remember how Nick committed his life to the Lord and now, because of his commitment, you and I are able to embrace."

KGB agents constantly threatened everyone's peace of mind. Dressed like Christians, complete with head coverings and hymnbooks, the agents infiltrated church services and other public places to keep tabs on what was done. Despite their camouflage, however, the Christians always seemed to know who was who.

While in Kiev, Alex made contact with Georgi Vins's family. Georgi had been arrested in May for being one of the chief leaders of the unregistered church.

Georgi's father, Peter, had been a RUEBU pastor in Pittsburgh, Pennsylvania, in the 1920s. Although he knew he would be persecuted, Peter felt God wanted him to return to Russia at about the same time Alex and his parents emigrated to America. Peter was exiled to Siberia in the early 1930s where he died in captivity as one of many Christian martyrs.

Peter was not the only one who gave Georgi a parental example of strength and godliness, however. His mother, Lidia, headed the Council of Prisoners' Relatives. The Council circulated information about their persecution to the outside world and sought support for prisoners' families.

Knowing of the Council's work, Alex delivered funds, clothing and other supplies to Lidia so she could distribute them to families whose primary breadwinner had been imprisoned because of faith in Christ.

Dr. Kmeta, a Ukrainian journalist, especially enjoyed visitng Kiev. While there, the House of Writers, a group of his peers, honored him with several volumes of poetry by Ukraine's poet laureate, Taras G. Shevchenko.

As he and Alex packed to go to Minsk, Belarus and then on to Warsaw, Poland, Kmeta said, "Alex, you're a younger man; maybe you can help me by carrying these volumes of poetry."

Alex agreed and packed the books in his suitcase, along with letters he'd been given to take out of the country and tapes he'd made late at night of Russians singing for use on "New Life."

When Alex and Dr. Kmeta attempted to go through customs, the officials cleared Alex but refused to stamp Dr. Kmeta's visa. Unable to negotiate with the customs agents and not knowing what to expect, the two men agreed to meet again in Stuttgart, West Germany.

After Alex left, Dr. Kmeta was stripped and interrogated for hours. Officials confiscated all his photos and notes, including his diary and address book. On the pretext that he was hiding microfilm, the authorities even dissembled his watch.

Dr. Kmeta could not understand why he was being searched and nearly had a nervous breakdown. He later learned that authorities believed he was taking articles and information to print in the West because he was a writer.

When he finally met Alex in Stuttgart, Kmeta was still visibly shaken. But Alex also had a story to tell Dr. Kmeta.

While waiting for his train at the railroad station, Alex had started taking a few final pictures. A government agent seized his camera and ripped out the film, warning Alex that he could be arrested.

On board the train to Poland, Russian guards marched brusquely through each car to check the luggage compartments. As Alex began filling out the questionnaires he'd been given, he felt himself go limp. "Suddenly, I realized that I had so many things that were forbidden: letters, magnetic tapes, books. Everything that I wasn't to do, I was doing."

Alex prayed silently, *Dear Lord, what shall I do? If I try to hide the forbidden items, the officials will probably find them anyway.*

As stern-faced special militia entered his car, Alex felt fear rise within him. Alex saw passengers' hands tremble as they attempted to produce the documents demanded by the soldiers.

Shaking inside with palms dripping cold sweat, Alex forced a smile as he saw a soldier coming toward him. Before the officer started interrogating him, Alex asked, "Whom shall I thank for this most wonderful experience of my life where I was allowed to come back to the land of my birth?"

Taken aback by a tourist addressing him first, the officer asked, "Where have you been?"

After Alex told him, the soldier asked, "How were you impressed?"

"It was all tremendous," Alex replied. "I didn't see anyone hungry or in *lahptee*" (a Russian word for birch bark wrapped in burlap used by peasants for shoes).

Alex's volunteering positive information must have disarmed the soldier because he thanked Alex and began to walk away. Alex stopped him by saying, "You haven't even looked at my passport or checked my exit visa."

"*Dah, dah*" ("Yes, yes"), the soldier replied as he returned to Alex. Then he quickly stamped Alex's visa and said, "Please come again," without even looking in his suitcase.

"I thanked him heartily," Alex says. "But to this day, he doesn't know why I was so thankful!"

It is not the suffering but the cause which makes a
martyr.

—English Proverb

CHAPTER 11

A GROWING HUNGER
1966-1975: New Jersey; USSR

ALEX RETURNED HOME FROM his trip to Russia excited
about what God was doing in his homeland and
re-energized in his commitment to reach the Russian-speaking people of the world with the gospel.

In addition to pastoring the Manville church, Alex
shouldered increasing responsibilities as SMS expanded. Growing numbers of requests to speak and a
constant need to raise support for SMS missionaries
demanded careful scheduling.

In the summers, Alex piled everyone into the
family station wagon to take them with him as he
crisscrossed America to fulfill speaking engagements.

"I know it's not easy to be missionary kids who are
always in church," Alex says. "That's why we tried to
make the trips fun, even if that meant Babs and I had
to take turns driving at night so we could stop and do
things of interest to the children during the day."

In 1969, SMS expanded its radio ministry by adding two thirty-minute programs in the New York City area. Alex's Russian broadcast on WPOW in Staten Island reached Manhattan where, it was reported, more Russian Jews were living than in Jerusalem. The second program was a Russian-Ukrainian program on WAWZ in Zarephath, New Jersey, which reached Russian immigrants in New York City and Connecticut. The program offered practical help to newcomers and invited them to send their children to camp free of charge.

Upset that the programs attracted so many listeners, a few Jewish leaders went to the radio station and demanded airtime in which they attacked Alex and his ministries in Russian.

Alex happened to hear them malign his work one day when they said, "Pregnant Jewish women had their babies ripped out of the womb by Protestants during the early days of the Inquisition. How could you send your children to a camp run by the offspring of such hate-mongers?"

Shocked by the allegations and concerned that they would ruin the ministry of SMS, Alex confronted the station manager to ask for transcripts of the program.

At first the manager said he couldn't provide them, but when Alex told him what had been said and threatened to notify the FCC about attacks on his character, the manager obtained transcripts and promised the station would be more careful in the future.

Alex then contacted the producers of the program. "Why bite the hand that fed you?" he asked. "We've bent over backward to find your people jobs, furniture and housing when they were new immigrants. Camp was free for your children. We've never proselytized but only tried to help."

By tackling the problem head on, Alex short-circuited false reports that could have destroyed his ministry. "I believe it was of the Lord that I happened to tune in and hear that broadcast and I am grateful that it never happened again."

By 1970, Alex faced almost impossible challenges in balancing his schedule between the Manville pastorate and the proliferating demands of SMS. Things were going well at the church and no one wanted him to resign, but Alex knew his heart had always been in missions. As the pressures intensified, he realized that everything he had done had prepared him to head SMS: his work with Russian people around the world, his radio ministries, his involvement with RUEBU, his years as a pastor and Babs's willingness for him to make the change.

It was a bold act of faith, since SMS still struggled financially. Alex was grateful that several friends and churches committed themselves to providing his support so that he could use all of the funds he raised for the national workers who ministered to Slavic peoples around the world. That freed Alex to provide leadership, oversee administrative duties, keep the lines of communication and support open between East and West, and speak on behalf of SMS.

In the fall of 1971, Alex, Dr. Kmeta and Mary Selody were allowed to organize a group of about fifteen pastors, missionaries and laymen to fly to Moscow.

Many things were the same as in 1965: Intourist and KGB agents examined everything the Americans brought and monitored every move. The Moscow Baptist Church, designed to hold 800, was jammed with 2,000 worshipers. The crowds again gasped with recognition and crowded around the group to thank them for coming and for proving that Russian believers had not been forgotten by the rest of the world.

Their gratitude made Alex weep. Church leaders further warmed his heart by telling him that almost all of those seeking baptism as believers had initially heard the gospel by radio.

They also reported that there were more than 40,000 little church cells gathered around radios, often hiding under blankets so they would not be seen or heard, since listening to anything but government programming was forbidden.

Alex accepted his part in the drama of redemption with awed gratitude. That God could use simple words spoken into a microphone to produce believers who could enthusiastically practice their faith despite constant oppression, harassment and persecution humbled him deeply.

The trip was not without its tensions, however. Curious about how pervasive Soviet surveillance was, Alex had placed special dots on his suitcases and then positioned them strategically within little marks on the floor before leaving his room. When he returned, he could see that the suitcases had been moved and the contents scrutinized. It was sobering—but not surprising.

The cloud of repression and persecution under which the Russian believers lived was graphically portrayed in Kiev.

Five adults who had grown up in Mary Selody's orphanage traveled all night to see her. They arrived two hours early and joined the people thronging into the auditorium. When they saw the one who had taken care of them, they stood to their feet and shouted, "*Mamochka.*" The moment vibrated with emotion. The KGB, however, did not share the Christians' enthusiasm and prepared to arrest Mary as a "foreign agent" because, in earlier years, she had taught Bible lessons to the children in her orphanage in Carpathia, Russia, thus violating the communist claim that children belonged to the government which alone should train them.

Someone high in the government heard of the plan and warned Mary that the "Black Crow" (the limousine that carted people off to prison in the middle of the night) would come for her that evening. Advised to leave immediately, Mary gave a quick farewell and escaped to Hungary with only the clothing on her back.

When the authorities arrived that evening, they demanded to know where the Christians were hiding her. Through their tears, the believers replied, "Why would we be crying if she were still here?"

Alex was deeply moved by the incident and the people's response. "Their faces reflected such deep love and welcome. They literally drank in every word spoken and were eager for more. Nowhere in the world have I witnessed a deeper hunger for God's Word.

"After the service, some just took our hands and without speaking a word, looked deeply into our eyes and souls, showing the unity and fellowship that grows out of suffering."

As Alex traveled from city to city, he gave the Russian people little gifts such as pens, razor blades, kerchiefs and gum. The people were glad to get the gifts, but they frequently said, "It's the Word of God we want. Don't you have a Bible to give us?"

Alex knew the believers wanted their own copy of the Scriptures so much that they would pay $50, the equivalent of a half-month's wages, for a used Bible if they could find one.

Alex's group had brought as many Bibles as possible and, in an attempt to distribute them fairly, left a few in each city. One man immediately tore apart the Bible they gave him. At first, the Americans were appalled, but as they watched him give a few pages to all the others who were waiting, they realized it was his way of sharing, a heart-wrenching reminder of their great desire for the Word of God.

Alex felt frustrated by the situation. He knew that other groups were smuggling Bibles into Russia and suspected that the ever-present hunger was growing because of the expectation that foreigners would bring Bibles. He had always brought as many Bibles as he could but felt he had to be honest with the authorities for the sake of the ministries he represented, his fellow believers in Russia and the God of truth.

Alex hoped that contacts he was helping to establish would one day lead to widespread distribution of Scripture. In the meantime, he tried to do what he could to encourage believers and remind them that they were loved.

Even though officially there to visit registered churches, Alex also reached out to help those being persecuted in the unregistered church. "We're all Christians. Let's work together," was his exhortation as he delivered $2,000 worth of fabric, salami, sausages, coffee, tea and money to Georgi Vins's wife so she could distribute it to the families of those imprisoned for their faith.

The 1970 report of the Council of Prisoners' Relatives showed that over 500 Christians had been imprisoned, including forty-four women. Thousands of others had been interrogated, including nearly 400 children. Many had been arrested and forced to serve short sentences of administrative arrest or pay large fines.[1]

Georgi's mother, Lidia, the originator of the Council, had been so successful in her efforts to collect and circulate information about the persecution of Christians that she herself had been arrested in December 1969.

Rather than crippling the movement, however, Lidia's arrest simply spurred the other wives and mothers to greater activity in publishing thousands of pages of documentation and appeals about the unfair treatment believers were receiving.

Alex marveled at their resiliency. He also noted that many more young people were attending services in all the churches.

"Negatives often become positives in life," he explains. "Although immersed in an atheistic, materialistic culture which worshiped man and taught that there was no God, the young people began asking, 'If there is no God, why does the government need to spend so much money trying to convince us?'

"Knowing that what they were getting elsewhere would not take them through the trials of life, they searched for answers and realized they needed God. Attending church, however, cost them the opportunity to go to college or to have better jobs.

"While that presented a difficult dilemma, many young people began attending services anyway because such restrictions just created spiritual interest and made them think deeper. As Slavs, they were familiar with persecution, so it challenged them rather than destroyed them.

"People can tell if our faith is real. In fact, people are watching to see if it's real. Saul saw Stephen's faith when he was stoned and later became a Christian himself. Persecution simply makes the Church stronger."

Alex was not alone in his analysis. Willard Edwards wrote an article entitled, "God Isn't Dead in Russia," in *The Chicago Tribune*. There he reported that *Pravda*, a well-known communist newspaper specifically complained that foreign broadcasting stations "pour oceans of radio waves on the Soviet people with sermons and religious services."

Russian radio broadcasts and newspapers exhorted "the party faithful to stamp out this reprehensible return to 'fruitless dreams of a heaven-reward.'"

Edwards concluded, "God is not dead in the Soviet Union after more than a half-century of massive indoctrination in the cult of atheism. He may, in fact . . . be more alive in some areas there than in many sections of the noncommunist world where faith in a divine power has become outmoded."

Such a conclusion demonstrated the persistence of the Russian soul's search for God and the power of gospel broadcasting to keep truth and hope alive despite great opposition. As one of the pioneer Russian radio programmers, Alex played a key role in the ongoing saga which continued to expand as the powerful transmitters of HCJB, FEBC and TWR allowed messages of hope and salvation to permeate the vast expanses of the Soviet empire.

TWR had an especially profound effect as Monte Carlo's five million watts of superpower boomed its signal into the population centers of western Russia. Its effect was dramatic, as it could project further than all the other stations put together, thus making it harder to jam. People in rural areas who lived far from churches were especially appreciative.

As director of Russian broadcasting for TWR, Alex's brother, Nick, played a major role in securing and transmitting programs. His wife, Rose, and others worked relentlessly to air quality programs and to provide follow-up from TWR's headquarters in Monte Carlo.

As a shortwave pioneer, Alex had produced his programs out of a simple faith born of obedience to God. Penetrating the Iron Curtain which separated the Soviet Union's 225 million people from the rest of the world had been a daunting task, but God had richly blessed the effort. Now letters and stories poured in.

A teenager from Moscow, where tens of thousands were said to be listening, wrote, "I am sixteen years old and a science student. Previously I bowed before the tree of knowledge, but you—through your voice—have begun to sow the seed of faith in my soul."

A Siberian farmer wrote, "Each day we leave the fields early so we will not miss your gospel programs. We all dress in our best clothing and gather around the radio set to worship God."

A twenty-year-old wrote from White Russia (Belarus): "I am diligently searching for God's truth. I like your broadcasts very much. They are reaching down to the most sensitive chords of the human soul and are filling it with the light of the gospel. I would like to know the Living Word fully and am asking you, if it is possible, to send me a New Testament."

A long-time listener from the Kirgizian Republic wrote, "We have been listening to your broadcasts since 1958. I wrote to you several times by registered mail and ordinary mail, but apparently you never received my letters. If only you knew how much joy your broadcasts bring to so many people. I know some who have become children of God through your broadcasts, as they listened all alone on a small radio. We listen to TWR morning and evening and, when the reception is clear, record your programs for those who are not able to hear them."[2]

Another creative outreach involved Operation Olympics at the 1972 summer games in Munich, Germany. Alex's brother, Peter, and his church, the Mandon Lake Community Church of Union Lake, Michigan, played a big part in spearheading the effort which involved distributing attractive Olympic packets containing literature specifically prepared to challenge the atheistic mind, a modern Russian translation of Romans by Dr. Kmeta and a Russian version of "Truth Triumphant," a Moody Bible Institute correspondence course. As before, demand exceeded supply.

Because seventy percent of Russians read in their leisure time, Slavic Missionary Publications published books and evangelistic tracts to deal with science, creation, evolution and truth, devotional books, a Russian Bible dictionary and *Halley's Bible Handbook*.

In 1975, Alex received his third invitation to visit Russia. This time SMS Field Representative Rev. George Boltniew, Rev. Nicholas Sylwesiuk and Alex boarded an airplane at New York's Kennedy Airport to fly to Moscow. En route, a young Russian scientist told George, "Fortunate is he who is able to believe."

As the men heard that phrase repeated throughout Russia, they sensed that people really wanted to believe but simply did not have enough knowledge of Scripture to be able to do so. Over and over they thought of Romans 10:17 which reads, "So then faith comes by hearing, and hearing by the word of God" (NKJV).

Despite the risks, the men took twenty Bibles and one concordance for each church they visited. Alex, as always, prayed fervently before the trip and then marveled as "the eyes of customs agents looked right at the Bibles but still let them go through."

In addition to speaking in packed churches as before, this trip was characterized by meetings to organize greater cooperation between the Russian Baptists and their American counterparts, meetings with officials of a peacemaking organization, seeing the sights of the Kremlin and Zagorsk and visiting Voronesh, a military city usually closed to outsiders.

The Voronesh church exhibited great strength with 800 members, fifty of whom were lay preachers. Many young people filled the services which was especially gratifying since the city prided itself on being an important industrial center with a large academic community made up of many foreign students.

Alex was particularly delighted to be able to travel to his native country, Belarus, by train. The services in Minsk also included numbers of children and young people.

A trip to the region of Brest, located just three kilometers from the Polish border, touched everyone. There, where nearly everything was still done by manual labor, a large number of Christians, some of whom had waited for the Americans for two days, greeted them with flowers at the train station.

Bulldozers had recently leveled their house of worship which meant they now had to travel eight kilometers to Voolka where they met in a small building built for 150. That day, 600 pressed into the meeting house while more than 2,000 gathered outside.

At the end of the service, Alex and his companions were literally carried by the crowd of well-wishers who wanted to shake their hands to express appreciation for their radio ministry.

As they were being pushed on like a tidal wave, Alex looked at a young woman whose eyes swam in tears. She said, "Only this past Monday night as I listened to your broadcast, I heard the voice of God and accepted Christ into my heart—and now I see your face!"

Those who attended the service represented only a small fraction of the believers in the area. Because their buildings were small, many who wanted to worship grew weary of standing in line, knowing they would never get inside.

Despite concerns about his doing so, Alex decided to visit the local *Oopolnomotcheny*, the Head of Religions and Cults, a practice he had started on his last trip. As Alex approached the office, he could see the *Oopolnomotcheny* pacing. He appeared to be worried that Alex would be upset because the church had been destroyed. Instead, Alex greeted him warmly and gave him a pen. The man's eyes immediately lit up. When Alex also gave him a gauze kerchief for his wife and gum for his children, he burst into profuse thanks.

Later, Alex learned that his meeting resulted in the church's being granted permission to erect a building many times larger than the one which had been demolished.

While in the Brest region, Alex was allowed to visit some of his relatives who lived in the surrounding villages and towns. Although he spoke Russian, he was required to hire a guide, a chauffeur and a translator. They, of course, were government agents who monitored everything he did.

As Alex met with his cousins and aunts in Kobrin and nearby towns, he recorded the tearful conversations for his mother. Then, since he was not allowed to visit Sopli, the village of his birth, Alex scooped some soil from his cousin's property in Kobrin into a little plastic bag so he could carry that home to his mother as well.

Before returning to America, the group shared communion with the believers in Moscow. As the service ended, a sea of white handkerchiefs bade the foreigners farewell, and innumerable handclasps told of the people's appreciation for the visit, the Bibles and the broadcast ministry that had nurtured them—and would continue to nurture them with God's Word—through dark days.

He who risks his life and hands it over to God will share in the life of the world to come, whether martyrdom is his lot or not; but cowardice is certain death for the soul.

—Sherman E. Johnson

CHAPTER 12

"DID YOU BRING BREAD?"

1975-1985: New Jersey; Norway, Finland, USSR

UPON RETURNING HOME, ALEX presented the little bag of soil from Kobrin to his mother. Natalie hugged it to herself and cried, "This is the closest I'll ever be to the soil of my home."

When she heard her relatives on tape, she wept. That night, she placed the little bag of native soil under her pillow, a reminder of her great love for her motherland.

That same passion filled Alex, propelling and sustaining him through a myriad of conflicts and challenges in his quest to reach his people with the gospel and inspiring others to participate by praying, giving and sharing.

In his role as executive director of SMS, Alex continued to advise and oversee a multitude of activities as well as travel extensively. Joined by a team of representatives from around the U.S., he provided assistance to new immigrants and ministered to the many Slavic people scattered throughout the United States. SMS also pro-

157

vided a support network for national workers serving as pastors for Slavic churches in Argentina, Brazil, Paraguay, Uruguay, Germany, Poland, Belgium, France, Italy, Israel, Australia and the Soviet Union.

In all that SMS did, Alex required scrupulous accountability: "We're in the work for what we can accomplish, not for personal gain," he told his colleagues. "That demands that we be absolutely honest before God and man. Every penny we are given goes into the work and our records are always open for inspection.

"The secret is faithfulness. People need to know that we are genuine so they can trust us to use their gifts in the area of greatest need. That assures them that their investment is sound.

"It's amazing how the Lord blesses when we do that. Then even little things added together become big."

During the 1970s, the world began to protest the persecution against Christians in the USSR. By the end of the decade, Soviet officials felt forced to soften their stance.

Sensing the new spirit, President Carter negotiated a prisoner exchange with the Soviet Union in 1979 which included the release of Georgi Vins. In 1980, Solidarity emerged as a free-trade union in Poland, the first such union in the communist world. Each gain generated questions about retaliation, however.

When Ronald Reagan assumed the U.S. presidency in 1981, he pushed for a massive military buildup. The communists responded by increasing their military spending. With the possibility of nuclear annihilation chilling hearts in both nations, Alex received a letter from Russian believers asking him to visit the Soviet Union again. Rev. Wasilij Shachov, pastor of the Evangelical Baptist Church of Passaic and secretary of RUEBU, and Rev. Theodore Karpiec, pastor and SMS West Coast representative, also received invitations.

When Alex's visa came, it was stamped, "For Religious Affairs," instead of "Tourist" as on other occasions. Aware of the opportunities and limitations which might lie ahead, Alex rallied Christians to pray. Their watchword became "Not by might, nor by power, but by my Spirit, saith the LORD of hosts" (Zechariah 4:6, NKJV).

The funds for supplies and travel poured in quickly. Because his visa said he was going for religious reasons, and because he remembered the Russians' great hunger for the Word of God, Alex boldly filled eight suitcases with Bibles, Christian literature, tape recorders and shortwave radios.

On May 29, 1981, Alex flew to Oslo, Norway, where he visited the people and churches who paid for his broadcast time on TWR. After that, Alex flew to Helsinki, Finland, where he visited a Russian congregation. The Finns became excited about Alex's special visa. Convinced that it gave Alex an open door to take in gospel literature, they insisted on getting a footlocker which they loaded with pamphlets and books.

The footlocker weighed so much that it took two men to carry it. Alex was charged $1,047 to transport it from Helsinki to Moscow. "I was grateful I had my credit card with me to pay for it," Alex says with a twinkle in his eyes. "And you can imagine how much literature we had, because, in all that luggage, I had only one change of clothes."

When Alex deplaned in Moscow, he met Shachov and Karpiec who had arrived a little earlier on their flight from New York City. The three scanned the lines going through customs and decided to join one where people were moving through with no searching.

Wonderful! Alex thought as he waited.

But when it was Alex's turn, a female officer asked, "May I see your visa and passport?"

As soon as she saw the special stamp on his visa, she asked, "Are you bringing gospel literature?"

Shachov, who had a small suitcase with a few Bibles, blank videotapes and gospel literature stepped forward quickly and said, "Yes."

The agent said, "We'd like to see it."

Shachov opened his suitcase.

"It's not permissible," the agent told him.

Alex spoke up, "Who said so? It says here we have special permission from the top of the government to visit churches. You don't expect us to come with empty hands, do you?"

Undaunted, the agent replied, "I must check with my chief."

As she talked to her superior in his office, Alex could see him shake his head, indicating he was not going to permit it. He came out with a notepad and began writing everything down.

Alex couldn't help thinking, *If they're making such a big to-do about this little suitcase, what's going to happen when they come to me?*

Suddenly he noticed a baggage cart. Alex picked up one suitcase, then another and another, and loaded them on the cart.

"I tried to look nonchalant," Alex recalls. "As I looked at the footlocker, I wondered what I'd ever do with that. When the time came, the Lord gave me supernatural strength and I just picked it up and put it on the cart.

"As I did, I heard someone shout, *'P'hai, braht, p'hai!'* ('Push, brother, push!')

"I managed to get the cart to the door separating the customs area from the waiting area where some men from the church pulled the cart through while I went back to the customs counter.

"If I'd thought about it, I'd never have done it. But God worked everything out and I just did what needed to be done without thinking.

"I still had my overnight case. So I went to the agent and asked politely if she wanted to check it. She rechecked my passport and visa and waved me through without even checking my overnight bag. "I didn't do anything behind their backs. What I did, I did right in front of them.

"We lost Shachov's little suitcase with the Bibles and videocassettes which the agents could resell on the black market, but it was as if God used that as a decoy. We felt as if we were witnesses not of what we through our own cunning were able to do, but of what God, by His power, was able to accomplish."

The desire for Bibles and Christian literature was so great that everywhere Karpiec, Shachov and Alex went, the question was the same: "Brethren, did you bring 'Bread' "?

While in Moscow, the men visited Mitishche, a site in the suburbs they hoped would one day house a seminary. At that time, the only Bible training available was through a small correspondence school which was allowed to enroll only 100 students for a three-year study period. Knowing how much they needed additional training, the Christians rejoiced in thinking about a possible seminary.

After spending several days in the Moscow area, Alex and his coworkers traveled to Baku in the Republic of Azerbaijan. Just miles from Iran, the population was primarily Muslim.

"As we watched the people, our hearts ached for them. They were so bound by religious traditions but so far removed from really knowing God!"

The house of worship filled early and many stood outside. The audience included many non-Christians and government officials.

When the pastor introduced the Americans to the congregation, he stated boldly, "These are the brethren whose voices you often hear over the radio, and now, whose faces you can see!"

After the service, they were interviewed by the local press and radio. In response to searching questions, such as "How can we have world peace?" Alex replied, "There can be no peace until He who came to be the Prince of Peace rules as Lord Supreme in the hearts of men."

From Baku, the group traveled to Tbilisi, Georgia, often called the Paris of the Soviet empire. Nestled in the valleys of the surrounding mountains, Tbilisi awed the visitors with its beauty and cleanliness. They found four active Evangelical Baptist congregations of Russian, Georgian, Armenian and Ossetian origin meeting in the same building at different times.

In the Ossetian congregation of over 1,500, there were just four New Testaments in their language and songbooks only for the choir. Alex determined that providing additional Bibles and hymnals in the Ossetian language should have high priority.

On the final day of meetings in Tbilisi, the three Americans were asked to participate in all of the Sunday services. The day started out at 9:30 with a service in Russian that lasted until 11:45. It was followed by the Georgian service from 12 noon until 2:15. Then, at 2:30, the Armenian congregation gathered to worship. At 5 p.m., the Ossetians gathered, and at 7 p.m., a second Georgian service convened.

Alex, Shachov and Karpiec were expected to preach at each service. "We just had to depend on the Spirit," Alex remembers. "We couldn't repeat ourselves because some people never left the meetings."

The group's final days were spent in Kiev where they were enthusiastically welcomed in packed-out houses of worship. Having been there on each of his previous trips, Alex felt as if he were returning home.

At the final service, the congregation waved their handkerchiefs as they sang "God Be with You 'Til We Meet Again." Alex says, "We thought of the great hunger for the Word of God we'd experienced and waved our handkerchiefs in return as a pledge that we would become even more concerned and involved in helping them."

When he came home, Alex wrote: "We must always remember that Christians in the Soviet Union have to function in an atheistic society. Religious activity is restricted rather than allowed to flourish openly as we see it in the West.

"At times we are prone to promote a Western form of evangelization in certain Eastern European countries, but we must believe and accept that believers know how to work within the society in which they find themselves. We can best help them by strengthening their hands through prayer and moral support! Their knowledge of our understanding of their problems and our not questioning their loyalty does more to encourage them than anything else we can do.

"May God grant us wisdom in the West in our enthusiasm and desire to help, so we don't add to their difficulties and needs."[1]

Neither a man nor a nation can live without a "higher idea," and there is only one such idea on earth, that of an immortal human soul; all the other "higher ideas" by which men live follow from that.

—Leo Tolstoy, *Diary of a Writer*

CHAPTER 13

OPENING DOORS
1985: Moscow, Kharkov, Kiev, Leningrad, Odessa

WITH MIKHAIL GORBACHEV'S ASCENSION to power on March 11, 1985, two Russian words popped up in the media around the world: *glasnost* (openness) and *perestroika* (restructuring).

People on both sides of the Iron Curtain asked, "What does he mean?" as the Communist Party head spoke of decentralizing power by allowing open elections, a more independent press and private ownership of businesses.

As people tried to project what would happen, Dr. Bruce Dunn, a pastor and fellow NRB Board member, asked Alex and Babs to host a trip to the Soviet Union for a group from his church in Peoria, Illinois.

While plans were being finalized that summer, the Russian Air Force shot down a South Korean plane they claimed had strayed into North Korean airspace. Bombings at the Rhein-mein Air Force Base in

Frankfurt, Germany, and in Rome, Italy, added to world instability.

Uncertainty and fear gripped the tour group, so Dunn called to cancel the trip. Although Alex had no idea where he and Babs would get the money for their tickets, he felt strongly that God still wanted them to go and told his friend, "We'll go even if we have to pay for it ourselves."

The next time Alex opened his mail, he found a letter from a friend from whom he hadn't heard in several months. It read, "While in church, we read a report in the bulletin about you, and the Lord laid it on our hearts to send you this check."

Amazingly, the check was for the exact amount needed for tickets and visas!

A few weeks later, as they were driving to the New York airport, Babs remembered a stylish Russian woman who had visited her. When Babs had complimented her on her wardrobe, the woman had said she made her own clothes. Seeing a flea market on the side of the road, Babs impulsively asked Alex to stop. "I'd like to take some pattern books with me, and they might have some," she told him.

For some reason, they did. Babs purchased the paperback pamphlets put out by the major pattern companies and tucked them in the outside pockets of her suitcase.

◊ ◊ ◊ ◊ ◊ ◊ ◊

When it was time to clear customs at the Moscow airport, Babs felt very nervous. This was her first trip and she remembered some of the stories she'd heard about how tough the agents could be. She also knew that Alex had brought five suitcases when each person was allowed only two. And, except for one change of clothes, his suitcases were filled with Bibles, literature, microphones, cassettes, concordances, songbooks and cassette players.

Alex and Babs tried to find a line where people were moving through quickly, but a woman officer called them over. The customs agent immediately asked Babs, "Do you have any literature?"

Babs gulped and said, "I have some magazines."

"Let me see them," the agent said.

Babs fished the pattern pamphlets out of the suitcase pocket and gave them to the officer who started going through them very slowly, page by page, one issue at a time. Then she took the booklets to another customs agent who also began scrutinizing them.

Sensing they might be interested in the booklets, Babs spoke up when the agent returned saying, "Please, you may have them."

The agent replied, "No, I can't do that."

Trying hard to hide her own fears, Babs offered again, "Please take them. I can get myself more."

The agent looked around to be sure no one was watching and then slipped the pattern books into her briefcase and waved Alex and Babs through customs.

Babs says, "I really believe the Lord led me to take the pattern books so He could use them to close their eyes to the other things we brought."

After going through customs at the Moscow Airport, Alex and Babs were driven to the Intourist hotel by a handsome young man named Sergei. As they conversed, Sergei looked at them in amazement and said, "Ninety-nine percent of the passengers I pick up at the Intourist office do not understand Russian. How did you learn to speak Russian?"

After Alex told him about his family background, Sergei asked, "What kind of work are you in?"

As Alex explained that he was a radio broadcaster, he noticed that the color in Sergei's cheeks began to drain away. Within a few moments, the once talkative driver became very quiet. "Is anything wrong?" Alex asked.

"Sir," Sergei answered, "you have brought me into a state of shock."

"How?" Alex asked.

"My mother was a Christian. Soon after she became a Christian, my father left her because of her faith," Sergei answered. "Later, she suffered a stroke. She was bedridden for the next twelve years of her life and had to be cared for. The only joy she had in those years was to tune her bedside radio to Trans World

Radio from Monte Carlo. When I heard your voice, I knew immediately that I had heard it before, for I sometimes overheard your programs when my mother listened to them.

"Two years ago, my mother died. As I stood at her bedside in those last hours she told me that she had been praying that God would send someone from a far country to explain to me about the peace she had in her heart. I'm listening to you, but it is not your voice I'm hearing. I'm hearing my mother's last words to me."

Alex, Babs and Sergei continued to talk about spiritual things until they arrived at the hotel. Sergei helped them with their baggage and then, while Alex stood in line to get a room key, Sergei shook Babs's hand in farewell, pressing something into it as he did.

It was a note asking Alex to call him that night.

The next afternoon, Alex and Sergei met in a crowded area and then walked to a children's park. "We met as strangers," says Alex, "but after discussing spiritual matters for more than an hour, it is my joy to say that we departed as brothers in the Lord. With tears streaming down his face, Sergei said, 'God answered my mother's prayers.' "

Alex and Babs collected many memorable moments as they traveled from Moscow to Kharkov, Kiev, Leningrad and Odessa, meeting Christians in many unexpected places: hotel lobbies, airplanes and public places.

As foreigners traveling with Intourist, they were the first ones to be seated on their flight from Kharkov to

Kiev. A young red-haired woman took the seat directly in front of Alex and began talking with an American sitting across the aisle from her. The American had studied Russian while a university student, but his vocabulary was limited, so he asked Alex to help translate when the conversation lagged.

As he translated, Alex learned that the woman, named Osya, was a doctor who practiced in the countryside near Kharkov. When she and the other American finished speaking, Osya looked at Alex. Somewhat embarrassed, she asked shyly, "Forgive me for being so bold, but are you Aleksei Pavlovich Leonovich?"

Alex was stunned. *Who is she?* Alex thought to himself.

"Do you broadcast over Trans World Radio from Monte Carlo?" she continued.

In his surprise, Alex blurted out, "Would you be a believer?"

"Yes!" she responded, grabbing Alex's arm.

Alex smiled and said, "Yes, I am Aleksei Pavlovich Leonovich."

"I can't believe it," the young woman repeated over and over again. "Dear God, I can't believe it!"

She went on to tell them she had no place of fellowship where she lived. Her only source of spiritual growth had been the gospel radio broadcasts.

Alex quietly asked Babs to give Osya a little New Testament. Afraid of what would happen if she were caught, Babs opened her handbag and carefully wrapped the

Testament in a handkerchief. Then, with a prayer, she slipped it to Osya.

As the plane approached Kiev, Osya, smiling through her tears, asked to see Alex and Babs again. Not knowing where they would be staying, Alex suggested they try to meet in the center of the city.

Having only carry-on bags, Osya got off the plane and hurried into town. By the time Alex and Babs met her, she had purchased a gift for them in honor of their friendship. Alex and Babs also gave her gifts, which she accepted with joy and gratitude.

Later, while in Leningrad, Alex's relatives from Kobrin surprised him with an unexpected visit. They were radiant Christians and gifted church workers.

On Sunday, Alex preached in the morning service. Suddenly, a woman cried out, "I'm repenting." Many others did the same. Each time, one of the elders went to where the person was standing and knelt with them as they poured out their hearts to God.

Restricted from giving open invitations, the elders continually undergirded the services in prayer so that the Holy Spirit would work. God honored their prayers even though those making public professions of faith knew they could become targets of harassment or persecution.

After the service, Alex met with the church elders, pastors and itinerant preachers who "picked his brain" on biblical subjects, especially prophecy and end times. They also told him that eighty-five percent of the 15,000 who were baptized in 1984 reported they were first introduced to the gospel by Christian radio.

"Continue sowing the seed of the gospel, and we'll continue reaping the harvest," the church leaders told Alex before he left.

As Alex and Babs left Leningrad to visit the Russians living in Finland, they tried to join a group going through customs. Young officers picked them out and ordered Alex: "Take everything out of your pockets."

When the search turned up a pen, they asked, "What's that?"

Alex replied, "You can see what it is. It's a pen."

Having already given out all of the Bibles and supplies he had taken as well as his suitcases, Alex had very little else with him. Nevertheless, the officials pulled Alex into a side room where they stripped and searched him thoroughly. As they went through his wallet, they found a $50 bill in a hidden compartment.

"What is this?" they asked brusquely.

Alex stared at the bill. It was a birthday gift he'd put in the secret section of his wallet for an emergency and then forgotten. Eventually he managed to convince them that it was an honest mistake and that he wasn't trying to conceal anything.

Meanwhile, other officials took a big vase Babs had been given and x-rayed it to be sure nothing was hidden in it. Then they told her to take off her wedding ring.

"I can't," she protested. "I never take off my ring and I can't even get it off."

The officers were not about to be put off. They waited and waited as Babs struggled and struggled to get the ring off. After watching her try vigorously for several minutes, they agreed that she couldn't remove her ring and finally allowed Alex and Babs to go on their way.

"They were unusually concerned and picky that time because some people had been smuggling gold out of the country," Alex explains.

Babs, however, didn't see it that way. She felt a tremendous strain from the ever-present surveillance which greeted them from the moment they landed.

"I was tired of having my every move monitored and my every word questioned. The rooms we had stayed in were comfortable, but we knew they were bugged. Going through customs was nerve-racking both times. It was little comfort to me to be told that it was better than it used to be. When Alex was searched and they wanted me to take off my wedding ring, I decided I never wanted to do this again."

Despite the negatives, however, both Alex and Babs felt that God had led them to make the trip. Taking the pattern pamphlets had opened the doors through customs. Alex's faithfulness in broadcasting the gospel had opened the doors of Sergei's and Osya's hearts . . . and thousands of others. The Bibles and Christian literature Alex and Babs had distributed would go on opening doors even though no one could predict where *glasnost* and *perestroika* would lead.

Even those who have renounced Christianity and attack it, in their inmost being still follow the Christian ideal, for hitherto neither their subtlety nor the ardor of their hearts has been able to create a higher ideal of man and of virtue than the ideal given by Christ of old.

—Feodor Dostoyevsky,
The Brothers Karamazov, 1880

CHAPTER 14

CRACKS IN THE CURTAIN
1985-1990: USSR; New Jersey

JULIETTA AND ROMEO MET while students at the University of Kiev and fell in love.

Julietta was a science major who hoped to be a teacher. Romeo, a secret believer since his early teens, was an engineering major who hoped to be a civil engineer.

One day Julietta said, "There's a rumor among the students that you're a Christian. Is that so?"

Romeo answered, "Yes, I am. I'm sorry I didn't speak about that before. Maybe I should have."

Julietta asked, "Well, if you are a Christian, how could we establish a relationship? Do you really love me, Romeo?"

"Yes, Julietta, I really love you."

"Then will you give up being a Christian?"

"Julietta, I can't do that," Romeo said sadly. "I love you, but I love God even more."

Romeo's declaration immediately led to his being expelled from the university with no chance to complete his education. Julietta graduated and married another man.

This true story became the basis for a radio drama on "New Life" which portrayed the cost of following Christ.

Persecution had become more subtle, but Russian Christians faced its reality daily, joining a long line of evangelicals who had suffered for their faith.

One year after Gorbachev assumed leadership in the USSR, people still wondered where his announced reforms of *glasnost* and *perestroika* would lead. Would they make any real difference? Would they bring about lasting changes or simply set up a trap to be sprung when everyone had openly declared his or her true allegiance?

In April of 1986, the Chernobyl nuclear accident shook the world. Everyone worried about fallout, both radioactive and political, for the Soviet Union and the rest of the world. This time, however, instead of following their usual pattern of denial, the Soviet government admitted responsibility and asked for help in coping with the disaster.

SMS joined with many other organizations in sending medical supplies to help care for those most directly affected. National workers visited hospitals to distribute supplies and demonstrate Christian love for those who were suffering.

The following year, Alex and Dr. Joel Nederhood, of "The Back to God Hour" radio program and "Faith 20" telecast, decided to visit the Soviet Union to assess the feasibility of producing a Russian version of the television program.

Travel was restricted and expensive. Alex and Joel finally decided that joining an American Express tour was their best option. Although Babs had said she didn't want to go to the USSR again, she relented in order to be a companion for Joel's wife, Mary Lou. The foursome flew to Moscow on June 26, 1987. As part of the tour, they traveled to Tashkent, Tblisi, Erevan, Yalta and Leningrad.

As before, wherever they went, they spoke in churches filled with attentive worshipers. Despite the pervasive, oppressive presence of KGB agents sitting in the balconies to oversee the services, many people stood to publicly repent and get right with God.

After the services, people pressed in upon the men, eager to meet the broadcasters to whom they listened. Many of the women also crowded around Mary Lou and Babs. One young girl especially impressed the women when she related that she had hitchhiked all night to attend the services.

Nearly everyone told how much they depended on the teaching and encouragement they received by listening to the Christian broadcasts on their radios. Babs became so excited about what she was hearing that she broke through the crowd to tell Alex how impressed she was to hear firsthand reports of how much "New Life" meant to the Russian people.

One evening, as the couples were taking a taxi from the Cosmos Hotel to the Moscow Baptist Church, the driver recognized Alex's voice and then asked who the other gentleman was. When Alex told him it was Dr. Nederhood, the taxi driver asked, "Is that the man who writes the 'Back to God' program?"

When assured that it was, the driver proceeded to tell them the times and stations where he listened while thanking them profusely for their broadcasts. Nederhood was so moved by the man's gratitude that he jumped out of the car as soon as it stopped so he could take the man's picture.

As the taxi disappeared in traffic, he turned to his wife and asked if she had his briefcase and Bible. "No, I thought you had them," Mary Lou replied.

Disappointed but unable to do anything about the situation, Joel consoled himself with believing that God must have wanted the driver to have the Bible even though it was in English.

After the service, the pastor invited Alex and Joel to his office. Before long, they heard a knock. When they opened the door, they saw the taxi driver standing there with Joel's Bible and briefcase. "I noticed them after I got home and was cleaning the cab."

Joel, with Alex as his translator, told the man how much he appreciated his honesty and his driving an hour to return the items. After giving him a gift, they asked him about his personal relationship with God. Before he left, the taxi driver also accepted another gift: the gift of eternal life.

Despite opportunities to meet with believers and to lead the taxi driver to Christ, the trip was filled with tension and fear. No one seemed to know what *glasnost* and *perestroika* meant in everyday life nor what it would mean for the future. The Communist Party remained solidly in control with Premier Gorbachev, an avowed atheist and a shrewd politician, at the helm.

Uncertainty and skepticism flourished. Although he had no idea what the future held, Alex felt Christians in both Russia and America needed to take advantage of every opportunity at this crucial time in history. With that in mind, Alex and Joel made contacts for producing "Faith 20" in Russian. Mikhail Morgulis, Nederhood's Russian counterpart on "The Back to God" radio broadcast, was selected to host the television program.

Morgulis was a natural, knowing just what to do, and "Faith 20" quickly became the most popular Christian television program in the Soviet Union. Joel's messages were geared to the universal needs of people; the Russian interpretation gave them such immediacy and relevance that people thought the programs had been made specifically for them. The messages were so effective that pastors began letting their congregations out early so they could see the program.

Meanwhile, health problems threatened to sideline Alex. A kidney stone wracked his body with excruciating pain and required hospitalization. Forced to cancel some of his speaking engagements, Alex became discouraged. His forty plus years of full-time ministry began to weigh heavily on him. "I didn't know how to relax and sometimes, especially when faced with particularly perplexing problems, I felt tired, discouraged and overwhelmed with the responsibilities of a very busy schedule and people looking to me to solve every problem, meet every need, pay every bill and energize every ministry," Alex admits.

As they drove to a regional NRB board meeting, he told David Virkler, a fellow broadcaster and friend, "Sometimes in my weaker moments, I feel like I'd like to quit. To just pack it all in."

Alex faltered under his load of responsibilities, but God kept right on working.

On March 3, 1988, a short article with the headline, "Moscow Lifts Curb on Bible Imports" appeared in Pravda. At about the same time, the Associated Press ran a story saying the Soviet government had announced that there would be no history exams in the USSR that year because the history they'd been teaching was incorrect. The radio report lasted only a few seconds, but it signaled a desire to teach truth instead of propaganda and led to a massive rewriting of Russian textbooks and literature.

Alex saw that new doors were opening and told American and Russian believers, "This is God's hour to do God's work, and we need to capitalize on it."

The Russians responded, "Give us the right tools and we will evangelize our people. Train us and we will do the job ourselves."

Alex took their challenge to fellow believers and churches in America. Convinced that it was more important to get the Scriptures in than it was to get Christians out, Alex encouraged Americans to travel to the Soviet Union that summer so that those going could carry in Scriptures and small tape recorders. He also called for increased production and distribution of Russian Bibles.

Despite escalating opportunities, however, Alex's health continued to decline. While taking his grandson Aaron to school on May 25, 1988, he made a wrong turn. Aaron corrected his grandfather and got him back on course, but Alex couldn't remember how he got home. Later, Babs found him staring blankly at the clothes in his closet when she came to find him for a phone call. As Alex talked to his daughter Deena, she realized he wasn't making any sense.

Deena immediately phoned her brother David and had him call their father. David also sensed that something was wrong and called Deena's husband, Ken, who was a doctor. Ken ordered Alex to go to the hospital where he underwent an angiogram, which showed a blockage causing global amnesia.

Alex was immediately placed on medication, allowing him to regain his memory two days later, but he and those who loved him were impressed anew with the frailty of human life and the inability to predict what any day might hold.

The next month, SMS's literature arm, Slavic Missionary Publications, together with Slavic Gospel Association, responded to the open door for Bibles by quietly sending 30,000 copies of a Russian version of the New Scofield Bible, which had been painstakingly translated and published in Ashford, Connecticut.

Plans were made to send 20,000 more within a few months. The German Bible Society, the Gideons and Campus Crusade for Christ also joined in the effort by sending Bibles to the Soviet Union.

"The Back to God Hour" organized a trip for late June. Alex was scheduled to host it, but his doctors would not allow him to travel. Alex asked Mikhail Morgulis (often called Misha) to take his place. While Misha spoke fluent Russian, his English was broken. Consequently, the group was forced to hire an interpreter named Larissa. Assuming that they would be interested in tourist attractions, Larissa promptly started making plans to take the Americans to theater and ballet performances.

Alex, his mother Natalie and his brother Nick left Sopli, Belarus for America in 1929 to join Alex's father Paul in America. Their emigration papers were some of the last to be approved before Stalin closed the door.

In February, 1945, Alex proposed to Mary "Babs" Babich, the young woman who said she would never marry a Russian. They were married February 23, 1947.

Alex spent 19 months doing evangelistic work in the jungles of South America while also broadcasting the gospel into the USSR via shortwave radio from HCJB in Quito, Ecuador.

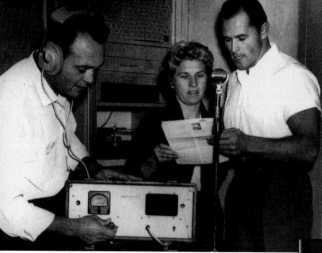

Alex adjusts the controls on a Magnacord tape recorder while Roz and Nick Leonovich assist in producing a program for "New Life" in 1954. The new equipment streamlined what had been a cumbersome process.

Mrs. Ivan Neprash officially turned over the leadership of the Russian Missionary Service (RMS) to Alex in January, 1958. (Her husband, the founder of RMS, died unexpectedly in April, 1957.) Alex asked that RMS be renamed the Slavic Missionary Service (SMS) to reflect its outreach to all of Slavic heritage.

Dr. Ivan Kmeta, president of Russian-Ukrainian Evangelical Baptist Union (RUEBU), and Alex visited the USSR in October, 1965. The visit was historic because it was the first time the evangelical church in Russia was allowed to host church leaders from America. For Alex, it ended 20 years of having his requests for visas denied.

A glimpse of the 2,500 people Alex saw when he preached in the Moscow
Baptist Church in October, 1965.

Russian men look at tote bags filled with Bibles and gospel literature on a stand set up by SMS near the entrance of the main stadium at the 1972 Munich Olympics. Those from communist bloc countries came at night and often eagerly took the materials.

Dr. Robert A. (Bob) Cook, President of The King's College and speaker on "The King's Hour" presents a commendation to Alex for 38 years of broadcasting the gospel in Russian.

Members of Alex's family in Gorodyets, Belarus appreciated
Alex's visit in June, 1981.

No smuggling, but lots of luggage! Alex stands behind the boxes of literature
and flannelgraph materials he carried into the Soviet Union in January, 1991.

Friends since they were students at Nyack College, Dr. Paul Freed, his wife,
Betty Jane, and Alex celebrate the dedication of the new headquarters for Trans
World Radio in Cary, NC.

On October 21, 1991, Premier Mikhail Gorbachev addressed a group of evangelical leaders (below) who were invited to dialogue with Russian officials as part of Project Christian Bridge. The invitation grew out of kindnesses Alex and Mikhail Morgulis, President of Christian Bridge, extended to Russian leaders who visited Washington, DC in January, 1991.

Members of Project Christian Bridge and the organizations they represent, L to R: Philip Yancey, editor-at-large, *Christianity Today*, Inc.; Alex, Slavic Missionary Service; Ron Nikkel, Prison Fellowship International; Dr. Joel Nederhood, The Back to God Hour; Dr. Lynn Buzzard, Church State Resources Center; Peter and Anita Deyneka, Russian Ministries; (back row) Dr. John B. Aker, First Evangelical Free Church, Rockford, IL; Richard Mason, RBC Ministries; John Van Diest, Multnomah Press; Paul H. Johnson, Moody Bible Institute; Phil Downer, Christian Businessmen's Committee; Dr. Brandt Gustavson, National Religious Broadcasters; Rev. Martin DeHaan, RBC Ministries; Dr. Herbert Schlossberg, Fieldstead Institute; Dr. Kent Hill, Institute on Religion and Democracy; Dr. John Bernbaum, Christian Collage Coalition; Dr. Billy Melvin, National Association of Evangelicals; Mikhail Morgulis, Christian Bridge.

Alex, newly appointed KGB General Nicolai Stolyarov and Mikhail
Morgulis, along with other Soviet officials and members of Project Christian
Bridge, pray together in Lubyanka, headquarters for the KGB.
Note picture of Lenin on wall.

November, 1991: Alex embraces villagers in front of the house where his Uncle Daniel lived in Sopli, Belarus. Alex was overwhelmed with memories of playing with wood shavings when, as a boy, he visited his carpenter uncle.

The interior of his uncle's home was converted into a house of worship when he died.

Alex visits the well where he and his mother drew water 60 years earlier.

He was thrilled when he was allowed to fulfill a lifelong dream of preaching in the village where he grew up.

Alex and his relatives rejoice in being allowed to visit with each other after decades of separation.

A variety of emotions are exhibited as Alex meets with friends and relatives in Gorodyets, Belarus in November, 1991.

A resident shows her delight at the large stack of Bibles sent by SMS for distribution in her area.

At the 1992 NRB Convention in Washington, DC, Alex receives a citation from Konstantin Lubenchenko and Mikhail Morgulis.

General Nikolai Stolyarov and Alex discuss plans to travel to college campuses in the American midwest so Stolyarov can speak and arrange internships for those who must retrain for new careers because of massive military cuts in Russia.

Inmates in a Moscow prison hold copies of Bibles they received from SMS, a sampling of the many thousands of Scriptures distributed to people in all walks of life.

The Baptist Church in Kobrin was built from old bricks retrieved from abandoned factories and glazed with a stucco made of crushed glass. Alex participated in the dedication of the church.

Part of the crowd that gathered for the dedication of the Kobrin church.

Basil Pavel, a Russian believer, served 18 years in hard labor camps because he distributed Scriptures. He credited Alex's preaching with helping to sustain him throughout his imprisonment. After his release, Basil built a church in Moldova and asked Alex to participate in its dedication.

Mikhail Morgulis raises his fingers in a "V" for victory as he and Alex stand in front of the Russian Parliament Building (often called the White House) where anti-democracy forces barricaded themselves in an attempt to wrest the government from President Boris Yeltsin. The top of the building was badly charred in the skirmish.

On October 5, 1993, the day after President Yeltsin's troops quashed the coup, Alex stands in front of one of the tanks.

Alex with General Nikolai Stolyarov and his wife, Yelyenna. Stolyarov was assaulted because he remained loyal to President Yeltsin during the coup.

Author Philip Yancey and Alex in 1994. Yancey participated in Project Christian Bridge and recorded his impressions of the visit in *Praying with the KGB*.

Alex translates for Anatoli Krasikov, President Yeltsin's press secretary, as Krasikov speaks at the 1994 National Religious Broadcasters' Convention in Washington, DC.

On April 29, 1994, Alex received an honorary doctorate in the fields of religion and philosophy from Friendship University in Moscow, the first honorary doctorate ever given to a foreigner.

At the 1995 NRB convention, Stuart Epperson of Salem Communications gives Alex the Milestone Award for 50 years of broadcasting "New Life."

Dr. Joseph Stowell, President of Moody Bible Institute, presents Babs and Alex with a citation celebrating their 50 years of full-time ministry.

Alex continues to beam the gospel into the CIS by recording broadcasts in the studio of his home in New Jersey. "New Life" holds the distinction of the being the longest uninterrupted radio outreach to Russia.

The Leonovich family, February, 1997.

Alex and Babs cut their wedding cake on February 23, 1947. Now, over 50 years later, their testimony is "Fulfilled!" Both of them give each other the credit for the joyous journey they've enjoyed sharing the gospel around the world.

"That's not the reason we came," they protested. "We came to visit our brothers and sisters in the churches."

Larissa agreed to arrange for a bus to take them to the churches. Never having attended Christian services before, she felt puzzled by the warmth with which the two groups greeted each other and said, "You say you just met on this trip, yet you seem like you've always known each other."

In southern Ukraine, the tour group watched younger Christians carry rocks to build a church while elderly ladies patiently straightened rusty nails because there were no new nails available for the project. When the group started to get off the bus, the Ukrainian believers approached them and asked, "Are you ready to meet God?"

Larissa responded, "No, but I'd like to be."

Within a short time, she was, and later she stood in the Leningrad Baptist Church to tell how she came to know the Lord.

While the group toured the Soviet Union, Alex experienced additional health problems which resulted in triple coronary artery bypass surgery on July 19, 1988, at St. Joseph's Hospital in Paterson, New Jersey. When told about Larissa's salvation, he said, "You can see the way God uses even the problems of life to bring blessing."

In the days following his release from the hospital, Alex embarked on a daily walking program in order to regain his strength. Because his body consistently produced the wrong kind of cholesterol no matter what he ate, Alex also had to be placed on medication to lower his cholesterol.

Although his physical pace had been slowed, Alex continued to stay in touch with Christians on both sides of the Atlantic. Everyone was thrilled with the new freedoms, but many questioned whether the changes were real or merely decoys which would lead to new persecution.

As a growing number of Russians applied for visas to emigrate to Western nations, Alex said, "There are some vocal minorities who want to get out, but most Christians want to stay. They believe in the sovereignty and purposes of God and are willing to suffer if that is His plan because they consider it a privilege to be identified with Christ in His sufferings.

"They don't look for sympathy. They just want to be faithful in the place where God has placed them because they know that faith under pressure becomes a louder sermon than anything preached from the pulpit. It's hard to understand what is really happening, but the opportunities are second to none."

Observers remained reluctant to predict the future of the Soviet Union, but those who understood Russia began to see slight cracks in the Iron Curtain which seemed to signal genuine change. As 1988 drew to a close, Gorbachev ordered those previously imprisoned for their faith to be released from psychiatric hospitals and prisons.

When the new year started, Christians throughout the Soviet Union banded together to pray and fast for their nation for the entire month of January. Prayer chains prayed around the clock. Churches sponsored prayer meetings which lasted three to four hours. Some prayed individually in their homes.

A quiet measure of seemingly little consequence, it went unreported by the media. Length or lack of news coverage, however, does not always indicate importance. Significant spiritual forces were at work jarring the Iron Curtain which had kept so many in bondage for so long.

When Alex visited again in May of 1989, he was amazed by what he saw: "I could hardly contain the joy of what we were witnessing. It's a new day for evangelicals in Russia.

"For more than seventy years, people were brainwashed to think there was no God. Now, many churches have been allowed to reopen. Over 500 new churches are being built. Young people are in the streets putting up posters and billboards to announce Christian concerts and meetings. Christian choirs are invited to be guests on radio and television.

"I preached every day, often as many as five times a day. The services were always at least two and a half hours long. I also met with the young people and choirs to answer questions. They always asked for

Christian literature and books and our mail is over-flowing with similar requests.

"We have seen more reforms and opportunities that we ever dared dream would happen. I believe it's the net result of many years of God's people praying."

In September 1989, Alex and Joel Nederhood returned to the USSR at the invitation of Russian evangelicals who asked them to lead instructional seminars for church leaders.

Dr. Nederhood gave lectures on Christian doctrine in Kiev, Odessa and Minsk with Alex serving as translator. The leaders demonstrated great interest and requested help in establishing a seminary in Odessa.

The men preached in Minsk and Odessa and then conducted evangelistic services in Rogachev and Gomel, poverty-stricken cities which had been destroyed in World War II. People were especially excited about the opportunity to engage in evangelism as it had previously been prohibited.

As they were preparing for their flight home, Alex and Joel discovered that the Moscow Book Fair was being held in an enormous exposition palace across the street from the hotel where they were staying. Alex learned that the Evangelical Press Association (EPA) had a booth at the fair where, for the first time, they were allowed to give out Russian Bibles.

"The Lord directed us to go through one particular door out of the fourscore (eighty) doors all around that huge building," Alex recalls. "As we entered, we saw a sign for Broadman Press, a division of the Southern Baptist Convention.

"We walked to the booth and introduced ourselves. As we were talking, a man nudged me and asked in Russian, 'Tell me, sir, is this a Bible?' as he pointed to a book in his hand.

"Seeing he had a Spanish Bible, I answered, 'Yes, it's a Bible.'

"Then he asked, 'Is it a whole Bible?'

"I said, 'Yes.'

"He said, 'Well then, maybe I could buy it for myself.'

"I asked, 'Do you read the Spanish language?'

" 'No,' he answered, 'but at least I would have a Bible in my house.'

"I was so touched by his sincerity that I said, 'Friend, you don't have to buy this Spanish Bible to be a good luck omen. The Bible is something that you have to read to know what the message is inside. I promise that as soon as I get home, I'll send you a Bible in the Russian language.'

"When he left, the brethren at the Broadman booth said, 'You should go down this long corridor to the very end where Madalyn Murray O'Hair is peddling her wares. You'll notice something very interesting: She's a lonely soul. Not a person is stopping at her booth. Instead, people are inching their way by the thousands to the EPA booth because it was announced that they will distribute 10,000 New Testaments.'

"We went to see for ourselves and it was exactly as the brethren had said. Madalyn Murray O'Hair looked absolutely dejected. When I peered around the bend, I saw thousands of people standing in line six and seven abreast, sometimes waiting a whole day to get to the EPA booth where the Scriptures were being given out. I thought the contrast would make an interesting picture, so I took out my camera and snapped the picture.

"Just as I did that, I noticed that there were people coming with floodlights and a TV camera. I waited because something just hinted that they might want to interview Madalyn Murray O'Hair.

"And sure enough, that's what happened. They stopped by her booth and set up the camera and the floodlights. I wondered what would be asked and what her response would be.

"The interviewer, microphone in hand, asked Ms. O'Hair how she was enjoying her visit in the Soviet Union and at the Book Fair. She responded that she was thrilled to be in a land that was sympathetic to her atheistic views.

"Then she said, 'In the country that I come from, they're nothing but a bunch of neo-fascists trying to cram religion down the throats of the people. They stop my voice and don't let my views be heard.'

"When I heard her say that, my Russian blood pressure went up and, without thinking, I came right close to the microphone where she was speaking and said, 'That's the biggest diabolical lie of any that I have ever heard. Nobody has ever stopped your voice. You're the one who is trying to stop the voice of the Christians.'

"No sooner had I said this than she let loose with a barrage of vulgarity. I stood there aghast. When she finished, I looked at her and said, 'Ma'am, if you were any kind of a lady, you wouldn't be using this kind of language.'

"That made her give it to me double-barrel. When she finished, I looked at her and said, 'Not even your family is sympathetic with what you're doing.'

"Again she blasted me with profanity as she asked, 'What do you mean? Why, my son is standing right here. He's investing $25-30,000 a year to help me with my publications.'

"I said, 'He may be, but how about your son who's a Christian and is embarrassed by what you do?'

"She talked about that son with great vulgarity. Then the son who was with her raised his fist and said, 'If you don't get. . . .'

"He didn't have to finish the sentence as I saw his fist coming toward me. He was a big man who must have weighed over 300 pounds. I thought, *I'm not going to get run over by this bulldozer*, so I pushed to the side, almost landing in the hands of the police who were there.

"I looked at them in surprise and said, 'Sirs, this woman is not at all representative of our country. She is totally out of order. This is not the picture of America that we want you folks to have. You're more tolerant than she, and I thank you for this new day in the lives of the peoples of Russia and the new opportunities you're giving the Christian community.'

"Then I said I'd like to leave a little memento with them and gave them books in Russian entitled *The Beginning of the Universe* and *The Existence of God* published by "The Back to God Hour.""

"The police took the books eagerly, but when they did, the crowd which had gathered came at us in an avalanche saying, 'Me too! Me too.' We gave out everything that we had within minutes.

"The most amazing thing was that the whole experience was televised and shown throughout the Soviet Union the following day and it turned out to be an incredible opportunity to show the contrasts between atheism and Christianity."

In November of the same year, the Berlin Wall crumbled, the Stalinist regimes in Soviet satellite countries collapsed and the Baptists in Leningrad were allowed to sponsor Luis Palau for an evangelistic rally in an open-air stadium. Clearly, things were changing and critical cracks could be seen in the once seemingly indestructible Iron Curtain.

Be not forgetful of prayer. Every time you pray, if your partner is sincere, there will be new feeling and new meaning in it, which will give you fresh courage, and you will understand that prayer is an education.

—Feodor Dostoyevsky,
The Brothers Karamazov, 1880

CHAPTER 15

REVOLUTION OR REFORMATION?
1990-1991: Moscow

"WHEN GOD'S PEOPLE PRAY, God's Spirit works."

Alex said it often, but as the decade of the 1990s began to unfold, he said it with increasing frequency. He also traveled to the Soviet Union more often. As always, Alex spoke in many churches and helped believers in practical ways. Now, however, incredible new opportunities also began to unfold.

In February, Alex attended the Evangelical Baptist Union's (AUECB) 44th Congress in Moscow where, for the first time, the Congress convened with full state approval at the Ismaylova, a large hotel built for the 1980 Olympics.

When Alex returned from his first two trips to Russia in 1990, he told Americans, "What I saw and heard made me exclaim time and time again, 'Lord, I believe, but help Thou my unbelief.'

"It is a new day in the Soviet Union. The changes are coming about with such rapidity that one can hardly keep up with the turn of events. In the churches, one can feel a stir and an excitement which couldn't be felt before. The new freedoms have opened the doors for new opportunities.

"Who would ever have thought there would be a day that I would be able to stand in Red Square, in the shadow of the mausoleum where Lenin's body lies, and preach the Word of God, give out Scriptures and gospel literature and witness to people personally in an open-air meeting?

"Who would ever have imagined that in our life-time we would see eighteen-wheel trucks from the West bringing in Bibles as well as a printing press and hundreds of tons of paper to print Bibles and gospel literature right in the Soviet Union?

"Who would ever have dreamed that pastors and musical groups would be invited to share the gospel in jails where Christians were once kept as prisoners for their faith?

"Who would ever have predicted that Soviet radio and television would eagerly air church services and messages in prime time or that Trans World Radio would be allowed to build recording studios in Moscow, Kiev and Minsk?

"Who would ever have envisioned how quickly Russian Christians would work to reestablish closed churches and build new ones?

"We weren't ready for this open door. We're working head over heels to catch up because we fear that the door could close just as quickly as it opened, and then we would be sorry we didn't do more. I feel utterly helpless because the task is so great. The opportunities are so many and we are so limited. I pray God will give us the personnel, the means and the wisdom to best utilize this opportunity."

Although Alex felt overwhelmed and inadequate, he responded with great urgency and peak efficiency as he plunged in heart-first not only to preach the gospel, but also to demonstrate the love of God.

As in the past, Alex not only supported nationals in their efforts to evangelize and plant new churches, but also actively networked with Western evangelical organizations to send badly needed food staples and medical supplies to a nation where the shelves were empty and the ruble badly devalued.

In October of 1990, the Soviet government passed the Freedom of Conscience Act which resulted in the release of religious and political prisoners who had been incarcerated in prisons and mental institutions. In November, United States President George Bush and Soviet Premier Mikhail Gorbachev proclaimed that the Cold War of over forty years was officially over. By the end of the year, all fourteen Soviet republics had declared that the laws of their republics took precedence over those of the USSR.

Yet despite all the sweeping reforms and official proclamations, Soviet watchers noted that the Communist Party, notorious for sudden changes of leadership, ultimately held the reigns of authority both in implementing policy and in enforcing it through the powerful arm of the KGB. Many cautioned that it was still wise to be wary.

In January of 1991, the World Culture Association, which included artists, musicians and intellectuals from around the world, asked Alex and Joel Nederhood to be their guests at a roundtable discussion on the Reformation.

The two Americans arrived early so they could meet with church leaders in Leningrad and Moscow. They also delivered four wheelchairs and large quantities of vitamins, insulin syringes and other medical supplies to the Moscow suburb of Reutov.

Tattered Russian soldiers met Alex and Joel in Reutov to help carry the supplies to the Komsomol building, where they presented them to city officials, who proudly wore Russian flags to indicate they were communists.

Alex announced that the supplies were given in the name of Christ. The city fathers accepted the gifts with gratitude, saying, "There are many people who promise assistance but this is the first group to actually give it."

After showing the visitors through their snow-packed city, the officials invited Alex and Joel to dinner. Alex said, "We always open our meals with prayer," and then asked Joel to pray. Joel reports, "I prayed a rather long prayer which included several items in addition to giving thanks for the food. Alex translated so that both our heavenly Father and those present would understand."

Later, they went to the auditorium of the Youth Komsomol League where they attended a concert by the Logos Choir, a member of the World Culture Association. The choir presented numbers which elicited responses of "Praise God," a phrase never before voiced in a building dedicated to extolling Lenin and the Communist League.

On January 13, 1991, the same day on which the World Culture discussions were scheduled, Lithuania declared its independence from the USSR. Tens of thousands of Lithuanians gathered in Vilnius, their capital, to demonstrate their desire for autonomy. Gorbachev responded by ordering tanks and troops into Lithuania to quash the demonstration. Instead of quelling the drive for freedom, however, the harsh response prompted Lithuanian protesters to march in the streets of Moscow, forcing the Intourist chauffeur to take many detours as he drove Alex and Joel to their meeting. The air crackled with political tension.

Concerned about being late for the discussion, Alex and Joel breathed a prayer of thanksgiving when they finally arrived at Moscow's prestigious Rachmaninoff Auditorium in the Tchaikovsky Conservatory of Music. As they entered, they noticed radio microphones and television cameras had been set up for nationwide broadcasting, indicating that the discussion would have a widespread impact.

Dr. Nederhood spoke to the elite group of thinkers and leaders for over an hour, giving them the background of the causes and effects of the Reformation and a grand history of God's involvement. He spoke fluently, without notes, while Alex translated.

At the end, the gentleman in charge of the discussion looked into the television cameras and said, "Friends, we can see by what we have just heard that the Reformation has never, never touched the borders of our land. Ladies and gentlemen, I realize today we need to go backward in order to move ahead."

His statement seemed to reflect the mood of the people across the Soviet Union who were struggling to rethink their past, look for truth and press for reform. Sensing the uncertainty that stalked the Soviet system, visionaries began to hope they could actually implement the openness and restructuring Gorbachev promised when he introduced *glasnost* and *perestroika*.

Lithuania prevailed, achieving status as an independent state. Other people from Slavic backgrounds who dreamed of reclaiming their heritage and establishing their identity cheered the courageous Lithuanians.

Alex returned to the United States just in time to attend the annual NRB Convention in Washington, DC. As Babs assisted with registration, she overheard some men speaking in Russian. They were quite disturbed, saying, "What should we do? Where shall we go?" Babs approached them with a smile and said in Russian, "How beautiful to hear the Russian language being spoken. Maybe there is something I can do to help you?"

The delegation explained they had come from Russia to meet with representatives from Holland who had chosen the Sheraton Washington Hotel as a neutral place to discuss the establishment of a children's fund to aid those involved in the Chernobyl disaster.

Babs called Alex. The head of the Russian delegation, Konstantin Lubenchenko, showed Alex a letter explaining the arrangements for the meeting. Alex determined that they had come to the right hotel, but upon questioning the hotel staff, learned that the Dutch group was not scheduled to arrive until the next day.

Realizing the predicament that the men were in, Alex immediately introduced them to Dr. E. Brandt Gustavson, Executive Director of the NRB, and Mikhail Morgulis.

Alex and Misha then showed the Russians around Washington. As they talked, the Americans learned that Mr. Lubenchenko had recently been elected as a deputy of the Supreme Soviet and that the other men also held high positions in the Soviet government.

That evening, Alex took the Russians to the NRB Anniversary Banquet as his honored guests and the next morning to a Presidential Prayer Breakfast where they met President George Bush and other government leaders. Impressed and grateful, the Russian officials carried fond memories with them when they returned to the Soviet Union. The courtesies extended to them while in Washington led to a growing relationship with Misha and Alex throughout the year.

In June 1991, Boris Yeltsin resigned from the Communist Party. He subsequently won the first democratic election for President of the Republic of Russia. Yeltsin's success cast a large question mark over the future of the Soviet Union because, while Russia was only one of fifteen republics in the USSR, it was the largest and most influential. Would transitions take place peacefully or would they erupt in chaos and bloodshed?

Despite the volatile atmosphere, Alex and Radio Bible Class (RBC) Ministry representatives Rick DeHaan and Dick Mason visited the Soviet Union in August 1991, to explore the possibilities of televising "Day of Discovery." The trio also delivered 30,000 volumes of a year-long Russian compilation of "Our Daily Bread" devotionals, the firstfruits of a projected run of 1 million hardcover copies designed to become library editions.

On August 19, just after Alex and the RBC representatives returned home, top communist officials opposed to reform in the USSR staged a *coup d'etat* against Gorbachev at the *dacha* in the Crimea where he and his family were vacationing. The revolt occurred just one day before Gorbachev and leaders from ten of the Soviet republics were scheduled to sign a treaty which would allow the republics a large amount of self-government.

Coup planners isolated Gorbachev by cutting telephone lines, then demanded that he declare a state of emergency or resign. He refused. In retaliation, the coup leaders blocked the runway at the airport, announced that the premier had been replaced for health reasons and shut down radio and television broadcasting.

Boris Yeltsin denounced the coup. Because of the media blackout, however, he had trouble getting his message out. Despite that, thousands of citizens risked their lives by joining hands to resist the advance of the coup's armored cars and tanks into Moscow. Yeltsin himself climbed on top of tank #110 and demanded that the country return to a normal constitutional government. Pro-democracy forces prevailed, ending the coup on August 21.

As soon as the crisis passed, Gregory Komendant, First Vice President of the AUCECB, called Alex to assure him that they were all well.

Alex asked, "Dear brother, in the face of all that's happened, how is the Church responding? Are there any aftereffects?"

Komendant responded with just one word which he whispered and then repeated progressively louder and louder until he was shouting: "Hallelujah! Hallelujah! Hallelujah!"

Knowing that meant that the doors remained open and that people were continuing to give out the Word of God at a fevered pitch, Alex replied, "Praise the Lord!"

Komendant ended the conversation with the request he so often made: "Just give us the tools so we can continue the work."

Spiritual vitality, however, stood in stark contrast to economic conditions. Alex reported, "While we were there, we were chagrined to see that the store shelves were empty. After all that's been said about a market economy, it hasn't touched the people at all."

Alex was drawn into the economic crisis when he received an official-looking envelope from the Soviet government. Worried that it was a summons from the KGB, Alex opened it carefully. Instead, he read that Lubenchenko, now Chairman of the Supreme Soviet, had been so impressed by what he saw and heard while in America that he and his colleagues were inviting a select group of American evangelicals to be guests of the Supreme Soviet to discuss the formation of a free-market society.

Alex was stunned. "Who were we to discuss a free market society?" he asked.

Alex called Misha who took the leadership in contacting individuals and organizations with an interest in Russian ministry to form a coalition which they named Project Christian Bridge.

In September, Alex and eighteen other evangelical leaders received personal faxes from Lubenchenko inviting them to come to Moscow in October. In part, their invitations read: "In the difficult, often agonizing transitional period that our country is experiencing . . . spiritual and moral values acquire a great, if not paramount, significance in their ability to guarantee us against confrontation, civil conflicts, the erosion of moral foundations and the lowering of standards. . . ."

Plans called for meeting with President Gorbachev and the Supreme Soviet to help the Soviet leaders "implement the moral values of Christianity" in their journey toward a free society.

When the American delegation arrived, they were featured on national radio and television and accorded red-carpet treatment, which included accommodations in the Oktyabrskaya (October) Hotel, once used primarily by top Soviet officials. They were also feted to private tours of Kremlin museums and other places of interest.

The Russians and Americans were seated across from each other at long wooden tables in the Grand Kremlin Palace. Members of each delegation introduced themselves and offered brief opening statements. Knowing how stridently religion had been persecuted under the communists, the Americans diplomatically asked for religious freedom, including the right to broadcast the gospel and distribute Scriptures without interference.

Anticipating an argument, they were caught off guard by Lubenchenko's response, "We need the Bibles very much."[1]

His only request was that they be given without charge so that more people could have them!

The major general in charge of the Ministry of State Security said, "In the past weeks I have been negotiating reductions in strategic nuclear weapons. . . . The cuts we have made will make our world more secure. . . . And yet I must say that this meeting with you Christians tonight is more important for the long-term security of our nation than the meeting between our nations' presidents on eliminating nuclear weapons. Christianity can contribute much to our security as a people."[2]

Other Russian deputies praised Christians for their help with the Chernobyl disaster, inquired about starting Christian colleges and asked about the relationship between democracy and Christianity.

Efforts to temper idealistic optimism with simple realism regarding a less-than-perfect American Church were consistently dismissed by the Russians, who declared that the underlying problem was spiritual and that Christianity held the answers.

Alex reflects: "I think they saw their ship was sinking, so they invited us in a desperate effort to get some idea of world opinion from those who could be trusted about what they would report. We met for an entire evening with their heads of government and had open, down-to-earth discussions of what their country really needed: a return to Judeo-Christian principles of morality and life. We listened to what they were saying and could hardly believe our ears.

"When Mr. Gorbachev arrived, he was totally different than we expected. He was very interested in what we had to say, and his entourage said they'd never seen him so relaxed. He was supposed to meet with us for just a brief time of about ten to fifteen minutes, but he stayed for almost an hour.

"I'm not sure how much impact we made on Mr. Gorbachev to change, but we gave him a leather-bound Bible with signatures from everyone in the delegation, a copy of Chuck Colson's *Loving God* and other Christian literature. He was very, very warm with us and received everything we had to say with a grateful heart.

"Before leaving, he told us that it was our spiritual heritage which had made our nation great. He also said that his mother was a devout adherent of Russian Orthodoxy and that his wife was more inclined toward spiritual things than he was. In fact he had said that his wife had told him, 'If you're going to have to break any other appointments today, don't you dare break the one with this Christian delegation who has come to see you.' "

Over and over, Alex and all the other Americans found themselves wondering if they were hearing correctly. As the historic day drew to a close, an attractive young woman, who was a deputy in charge of cultural affairs, said softly, "I am impressed with how freely you can talk about your faith. I envy you! We have all been raised on one religion: atheism. We were trained to believe in the material world and not God. In fact, those who believed in God were frightened. A stone wall separated these people from the rest.

"Suddenly we have realized that something was missing. Now religion is open to us, and we see the great eagerness of young people. I envy those young people growing up today who can study religion. This is a hard time for us, when our ideals have been destroyed. We must explore religion, which can give us a new life and a new understanding about life."[3]

Mikhail Morgulis, the organizer of the trip, responded by asking if the delegation could offer a prayer. His request was granted and everyone stood to pray.

When finished, the Americans walked out of the Grand Kremlin Palace as church bells pealed through the night, a sound silenced by the Bolsheviks until Gorbachev ordered them to ring again.

Ironically, it was October 31, Reformation Day. Change was sweeping the Soviet empire. Would it take on the character of the violent Revolution of 1917 or the inner transformation of the Reformation of 1517?

> The world would use us just as it did the martyrs, if
> we loved God as they did.
>
> Thomas Wilson, *Maxims of Piety*

CHAPTER 16

FORGIVING THE KGB

October-November 1991:
Moscow

THE LUBYANKA—MOSCOW'S MOST dreaded prison and the infamous headquarters for the KGB!

The very thought of visiting the Lubyanka made Alex and the other members of the American delegation shiver inwardly. Invasive terrorist tentacles had enveloped and imprisoned so many in forced labor camps, mental hospitals and other correctional facilities that statistics staggered under the volume, leaving estimates vacillating between 10 and 70 million.

Stories of inadequate food, insufficient clothing and inhumane cruelty resulting in indescribable suffering and death seeped out despite stringent controls and severe penalties. Some were whispered; some merely communicated by grief-ridden spirits. Few families escaped the pain and terror of nearly seventy years of totalitarian dictators who protected their power by force. An invitation to meet in the master control center for such oppression and torture filled the Americans with apprehension.

Alex relates his experience: "When told we would have a meeting at the headquarters of the KGB, I had great misgivings. Of all places! That was the last place in the world I wanted to go.

"For the twenty-five years I'd been coming to Moscow, whenever I saw that building I crossed to the other side of the street. I didn't even want to walk by it because it spelled hurt, tears and weeping to me since tens of thousands of believers had been exiled to Vorkuta, the most dreaded of labor camps in Siberia from this building. Among them was my mother's brother, and I felt bitterness and anger because of all it represented.

"Suddenly, however, I found myself inside that squat, gray fortress. Stone-faced KGB agents guarded the doors as we entered a wood-paneled room decorated only with pictures of Lenin and Feliks Dzerzhinsky, the terrorist head of the original hated secret police known as the Cheka.

"We were seated at long tables facing the head table. Cold chills went up and down my spine as I realized I was in the very place where others had sat in judgment over my fellow brothers and sisters in Christ.

"An aide to Gorbachev introduced KGB General Nicolai Stolyarov. His name meant nothing to me until we learned that during the August coup against

Gorbachev, Stolyarov, then a captain in the Air Force, had risked his life to fly to the *dacha* where Gorbachev, his wife, Raisa, and their family were under house arrest. He was in the cockpit of the plane which flew Mr. Gorbachev back to Moscow.

"Because of Stolyarov's heroic act, Gorbachev promoted him to general of the KGB. I relaxed a little as I realized that the man who would address us had not been the one directly responsible for the KGB's horrendous crimes against innocent people.

"When Stolyarov entered the room, I was surprised at how young he was. His warm smile put us at ease. As he looked around the room, however, he couldn't find his interpreter. So he asked, 'Is there anyone here who could translate for me?'

"All fingers pointed directly to me.

"My immediate response was, *Dear Lord, no!* but God's answer was *Yes*.

"I can still feel the emotion of the moment as I walked up behind that oak railing and those oak desks where godless, atheistic judges and KGB officers had pronounced such harsh sentences. Gorbachev's chief adviser in the field of Culture and Religion and current KGB officials were already seated at the head table.

"I stood to the right of General Stolyarov and began interpreting for him as he told of seeing parallels to the death and resurrection of Christ in the resolution of the coup against Gorbachev.

"Then he verbalized the irony of the moment as he said, 'Meeting with you here tonight is a plot twist that could not have been conceived by the wildest fiction writer. Friends, I wish to speak to you today on the subject of repentance.'

"Even as I interpreted his words, I prayed, *Lord, am I hearing right? Am I saying the right thing? Please help me translate his words and emotions properly.*

"I quickly turned my attention back to translating as I heard the general apologize by saying, 'We are sorry for what happened in past years, but that's gone and there's nothing we can do about it. Friends, we're living in a new day, building for a greater, better tomorrow.'

"As General Stolyarov spoke to us from his heart, he referred to a popular anti-Stalin film for which people had stood in line a few years before entitled *Repentance*. It chronicled the persecution, false charges, brutal imprisonment and demolition of churches which made people fear and despise the KGB.

"In answer to a question from our group about what changes the KGB planned to make, Stolyarov answered, 'There can be no *perestroika* apart from repentance. The time has come to repent of that past. We have broken the Ten Commandments and for this we pay today.'

"When Stolyarov finished, Misha said, 'General Stolyarov, as you recognize, we are here as a Christian delegation. We would like to give you a Bible and some Christian literature as a memento of our visit. Even more than that, however, we would like to have a time of prayer in this chamber.'

"General Stolyarov responded, *'Pozhalooysta'* ('Please').

"Misha prayed first in Russian. Then I prayed in English. When I opened my eyes and looked at the general, his eyes were wet with tears and I felt the Spirit of God must be dealing with his heart.

"In that second, I took him by the hand and said, 'General Stolyarov, first of all, I want to commend you on the speech you have just made, but I would also like to speak of another biblical word: *forgiveness*. I had anger and bitterness in my heart every time I saw this building because of the many innocent victims who left these halls, among them my own uncle who never returned to his family's side but died a martyr's death in Siberia for his faith.'

" 'Sir, as God in Christ has forgiven me, I want to say with every ounce of emotion and sincerity, I forgive you and the system that perpetrated all this.'

"Then something happened that I never anticipated. General Stolyarov looked at me with eyes that went deep into my heart and suddenly I found myself in his embrace as he kissed me on the right cheek and said quietly, 'Aleksei Pavlovich, only twice have I prayed and cried in my life. The first time was when I buried my mother; today is the second time.'

"He took me by the hand and gripped it hard. And deep within my heart, God also did a work. For when I said from the heart, 'I forgive you,' it was as if a burden was lifted, even though I had never fully recognized its presence.

"Today I thank the Lord for speaking to my own heart. Before we can do something for someone else, that kind of work has to be completed in our own lives. As I looked into General Stolyarov's face, it was with a different spirit because the power of God's Holy Spirit works in us to empower us to do what in the energy of the flesh we could never do."

That night, national television showed KGB officials standing with bowed heads as Misha and Alex prayed. The next day, newspaper headlines announced, *"Moleetva nah Lubyankje"* ("Prayer in Lubyanka").

The article touted this as the first time there was prayer in the Lubyanka, but Alex shook his head and said, "That's not really the first time there was prayer in the Lubyanka. Thousands and thousands of my brothers and sisters have wept to God from the cells below. I am honored to be a witness of history in the making as God now answers the prayers of these, His people."

Hundreds of thousands of believers throughout the vast Soviet empire no doubt felt the same way. Some remembered family members who had cried out to God from the cold cement cells; some remembered long days and nights when they themselves had pleaded for God's intervention.

Basil Paley had been one of them. When he heard the radio reports of the meetings between the American Christians and the government officials, he boarded a night train in Kishenev, Moldova, and rode fourteen hours to Moscow to see for himself.

Upon arrival, he asked where the American delegation was staying. Flabbergasted when he learned the group was staying at the Oktyabrskaya Hotel, he nevertheless located both the hotel and the room where they were gathering to pray and discuss the day's schedule. Unexpected, unannounced and unknown, Basil knocked on the door.

"When we opened the door," Alex recalls, "who should stand there but a broad-shouldered man with disheveled hair all over his face, two missing front teeth and a look of bewilderment on his face?

"After looking at the whole group, he spotted me and, almost like a locomotive, came charging at me and kissed me eighteen times on my cheek, saying in a bullhorn voice, 'Brother Alex, this is for every year that I spent in prison for my faith.'

"I looked at him in amazement. In shock, really. I had never seen him before. I knew nothing about him. I'd never met him.

"Then, through tears, he told me his story: 'Yours was the last face that I saw; the last message that I heard before I was exiled into Siberia. " 'In the 1960s, I was living in Ukraine where I was sought by the government for printing gospel literature on a lit-

213

tle press I had made out of washing machine parts. I distributed 700,000 little leaflets and gospels house to house in different areas during the darkness of night so I wouldn't be seen or heard.

" 'I had been in prison before and would have been arrested again if I had attended church, so I did my growing by listening to your radio broadcast. When I heard you were going to be in Kiev in 1965, I wanted to hear you in person so much that I decided to risk coming to hear you.

" 'As you know, every service was monitored by the KGB and everything was carefully scrutinized. Even though I was far from my home, the secret police recognized me, arrested me as I left the service and took me to prison. From there, I was exiled to Vorkuta where I spent eighteen years at hard labor. Yours was the last face I saw and yours was the last message I heard from the pulpit before I was sent to Siberia.

" 'You preached about Christ asking Peter the question, "Lovest thou Me?" Every time it got so unbearably hard and difficult in prison that I felt almost forgotten not only by man but even by God, I would see your face and hear you speaking that question. It was as if Christ was asking Peter—and me—"Lovest thou Me?"

" 'Then I would lift my head toward heaven and say, "Lord, You know all things; You know that I love You."

" 'For a while, I couldn't figure out why God would allow me to be punished for serving Him. Then, one morning, I saw that God had provided a new way to serve Him.

" 'Each day, we had to line up long before the sun came up. Prisoners had to be prompt, but guards did not. That meant that thousands of us stood outdoors with nothing to do. I decided to use those minutes to preach. I asked the guards for permission and they said I could if I would agree to do the filthiest job . . . clean the toilets.'

"Basil spoke with such force and animation that I grabbed his flailing arms several times as I pleaded with him to speak softer and slower so I could translate what he was saying into English. It was to no avail. He would lower his head and try to speak slower and more quietly, but within seconds, he would again be shouting like a machine gun. I soon learned why.

" 'In the beginning, I became hoarse as I tried to be heard by all the thousands of prisoners standing in line. Then, gradually, my voice became stronger. I never knew if I would have even two minutes in which to preach, so I learned to speak at top speeds and loud volumes. Sometimes it took two weeks to complete one sermon.

" 'But I've been back, and there's still a community of about 100 believers worshiping in that camp,' Basil told us, bathing us in the warmth of his enormous, crooked smile."

After his mother died, Basil began renovating her house into a church. It had taken many years, but he had finally finished. His trip to Moscow was not only to see firsthand what was happening, but also to ask Alex to speak at the dedication of the church.

"There were many years when I had no encouragement," Basil told the group. His voice cracked and he wept openly. "The words of this man, Brother Leonovich, I carried in my heart. He is the one who encouraged me when my hands were tied behind my back.

"And now, I can hardly believe the changes. To think that you are here in Moscow, the center of unbelief, talking and drinking tea with the leaders of our country. It is a miracle!

"Brothers and sisters, be bold! You are lifting up the children of the Lord. Where I come from the believers are praying for you at this minute. We believe your visit will help reach our country for God. May God bless you all."[1]

Alex and the other Americans represented many ministries. Together they had taken the gospel to countless millions around the world, by both spoken and written word. As they stood to pray with Basil, however, they felt humbled, knowing they were meeting with one of God's choicest saints, a unique spokesman for the millions of believers who had been persecuted for their faith in endless ways through endless centuries.

That evening, after an elaborate banquet at the Ukrainian Embassy, the group participated in discussions at the Journalists' Club of Moscow. The American delegation expected tough questions. Instead, when Ron

Nikkel, President of Prison Fellowship International introduced himself and told of Christ's power to transform prisoners, they applauded.

"What is this forgiveness?" they asked. "How can we find it? How do you get to know God?"[2]

They were also very receptive to Alex's observation that "Only the person who has made his peace with God can live in real peace with his neighbor," and to another delegate's statements regarding democracy and religion.

After the Americans had all introduced themselves, a distinguished editor of the prestigious *Literary Gazette*, responded by saying, "No doubt you know of the problems in our country. I tell you, however, that the greatest problem is not that we don't have enough sausages. Far worse, we don't have enough ideas. We don't know what to think. The ground has been pulled out from under us. We thank you deeply for coming to our country and holding before us morality and hope and faith. It is beautiful to see you in this place. You represent exactly what we need."[3]

A bald-headed dissident with bushy eyebrows and a bad stutter shouted, "You are our salvation, our only hope! We had a lawful country, a society with religious beliefs, but that was all destroyed in seventy years. Our souls were su-su-sucked out. Truth was de-de-destroyed. In the last stage, which we have just lived through, even the c-c-c-c-communist morale was destroyed."[4]

Startled by their insatiable interest, Philip Yancey later wrote in his book *Praying with the KGB*, "As in previous meetings, we tried to mention flaws in American society and in the American church, but the journalists seemed altogether disinterested in apologies or critiques. They seemed, rather, starved—grievously starved for hope."[5]

Basil watched from the back row of the theater. Each time someone mentioned God or Jesus, he raised both fists over his head as if to cheer them on.

Yancey realized that the Americans were Basil's "ambassadors, going where he would not be invited, speaking words he could not always follow, opening doors he had thought sealed shut forever. We, too, those of us who felt so unworthy in his presence that morning, had a role to play."[6]

Alex had been unaware of the role he'd played in Basil's life. Now, as he watched Basil cheer, he thought of Basil's important, but little known, role as one of the persecuted faithful who had outlived the Lubyanka by overcoming his unjust punishment with forgiveness and faithfulness. Alex wondered if he would have been able to do the same. Although Basil's request for Alex to participate in the dedication of the church cost hundreds of dollars and a change of plans, Alex's question for himself and others was the same: "How could I possibly turn down Basil's invitation?"

At the foot of every page in the annals of nations may be written, "God reigns."

—George Bancroft

CHAPTER 17

BACK TO SOPLI
November 1991: Sopli, Belarus

NEWS OF THE AMERICAN Christians' meetings with President Gorbachev, the Supreme Soviet and General Stolyarov commanded great interest as word spread throughout the Soviet empire. The coverage on state television and in sanctioned newspapers gave the group instant recognition wherever they went. Alex noticed the changes immediately:

"Suddenly we had more liberties in Russia than we did in the United States. Government officials gave us access into the public school system throughout the whole fifteen republics of the Soviet Union. We were invited to teach the Bible in the classrooms, especially the Ten Commandments. The teachers and the school principals wanted every child to have a Bible and wanted to include Christian literature in the libraries.

"We showed them a Russian edition of a children's Bible and told them we had printed 50,000 copies. They said, 'That's not enough. We need 15 million.'

"We showed them flannelgraph stories and they became excited and wanted them.

"We were invited to debate atheists on television. We were given prime time for radio broadcasts. We were getting a whole lot more for the dollar than you can imagine.

"I was embarrassed by our own lack of faith. We'd prayed for years, but when it happened, we were not ready with supplies or funds or personnel. With God's help, we quickly did all we could to make up time. We heard Jesus saying, 'I must work the works of Him who sent Me while it is day' (John 9:4, NKJV)."

The majority of those in Project Christian Bridge returned to the United States to report on their trip. Alex and Misha, however, stayed behind to participate in the dedication of Basil's church.

Ironically, in an unexpected twist, it was not to be. After paying the additional fees to extend his stay, Alex learned that the dedication ceremony at Basil's church would be delayed because the government insisted on various changes in the building before issuing an occupancy permit.

Alex's willingness to extend his visit, however, led to the fulfillment of a lifelong dream. For years, his requests to visit Sopli, the village where he was born, had been refused. Now, in a total reversal, authorities urged Alex to return to his birthplace, complete with a crew from Moscow's Channel 4 to videotape the visit!

"For years it seemed impossible to even think that my childhood prayers of returning to Sopli would ever be answered. I had been considered a traitor to the motherland . . . as one using religion as a tool for promoting capitalism. Now the authorities seemed to understand that I had tried to help the Soviet people.

"They were especially impressed that we had provided funds to help the children affected by the Chernobyl disaster. That was publicized and I received a letter of commendation from Mr. Gorbachev and other government leaders. But to think that they wanted to do a news report for television on the village of my birth was overwhelming.

"When we took a barge across the wide canal, I had an immediate flashback in which I remembered everything as if it had happened the night before: the cable-operated barge which got us from our village to the mainland, the wagon and horse we used to travel to the canal, net fishing in the canal, the time I launched a rowboat when I was five. . . .

"I looked at the barge with fresh eyes. The one we were on had a motor and was ten times bigger than the one of my childhood, which operated by a winch powered by people who grabbed the steel cable with their bare hands and pulled the barge from one shore to the other.

"As the barge neared Sopli, the villagers assembled to see who was coming. I was so touched by them. They were all very old peasants who wore boots and simple clothes. There were no young people because there was no work and no future.

"The villagers looked at the people and cars on the barge and asked, 'Who are you? Why are you here?'

"I answered, 'Does the name Leonovich mean anything to you?'

" 'Oh, they left for America years ago,' they answered in mixed Russian, Ukrainian and Polish.

" 'I'm the Leonovich boy who left,' I said. 'Now I'm returning as a grandfather.'

" 'Are you Alex?' they asked as they hugged and kissed me, surprise showing in their eyes. 'You're not ashamed to have us hug you? Aren't you embarrassed to kiss us old people?'

" 'No,' I told them. 'To me you're very precious.'

"They were very excited. In those moments, I felt their calloused hands and the coarseness of their grip and looked at the deep furrows in their faces and the shabby clothing on their gnarled bodies. It was such an emotional experience that we couldn't speak. Instead, we just fell on each other's shoulders and wept like little children.

"The whole experience was overwhelming. As I looked around, it was as if time had stood still. The ruts in the road were just where they used to be. The fences leaned just as they did when I was a boy. The flowers still grew on the thatched roofs of the little buildings which stood just as they did nearly seventy years ago.

"The only changes were the new barge and an electric line which provided a bare electric bulb hung from a chain in the center of a room instead of the kerosene lamps we had used when I was a child. My parents' house was gone, but not the well where we got water. I went to the well and dropped the rope so the poles would shift to allow the old galvanized bucket to fall to the water below. Then I lifted the bucket and began to lap the water like I had done as a child.

"Afterward, we went to my uncle's home where I spent so much time as a little boy. As the villagers gathered together in my uncle's home, I opened the Word of God to tell them that the same God who had made a difference in our lives could make a difference in theirs if they would give themselves to the Lord.

"I had prayed for years to be able to preach the gospel on the soil of my childhood. I was experiencing the answer to those prayers. Everyone cried and some of the villagers told me they already believed in God and called themselves Christians.

"As I looked at these dear people who barely eked out an existence with the most ordinary kind of work, I realized why the government had refused my requests for so many years: They didn't want me to see that there had been virtually no progress of any kind in the village. As I saw the closest of my kin still living in such poverty, I asked myself why I had been given so many blessings in America.

"All I could think of was Joseph who had also been a stranger in a strange land with a foreign language and culture. At times, he must have felt forgotten by family and even by God as he looked at the circumstances through which he had to live, but God was actually preparing him for a position of leadership so he could provide for his family during a time of great famine.

"As I looked at my relatives, I felt a great love for my people, a love that had burned strong through the years, and a great sense that God had called me to share my blessings with them."

The TV report on Alex's trip to Sopli, originally intended to be a fifteen- to twenty-minute documentary, was expanded to over an hour in length and was entitled "Fate." It was shown three times over the national cable network, reaching all fifteen republics in all eleven time zones. Gorbachev requested a copy for his own file.

For Alex, the privilege of going back to Sopli capped off a trip which seemed like a fairy tale. But it was a fairy tale that was still being written. Questions loomed for which no one knew the answers. Would the new openness to Christ continue or be crushed? Did government officials really yearn for spiritual and moral changes, or were they simply feigning interest before brutally crushing their unsuspecting prey? What was the best course for evangelical ministries to take?

The real question came down to fear or faith.

Members of Project Christian Bridge chose faith. Upon returning to the United States, they shared the urgency of the moment. Many ministries responded enthusiastically. The Gideons sent massive quantities of Bibles, then struggled to keep up with replacing Bibles in hotels as they were constantly taken.

Campus Crusade sent workers to prepare a curriculum on Christianity for the schools. Young Life inherited camps which had belonged to the communists. Focus on the Family negotiated releases on 2,500 radio stations, more than in the rest of the world combined.

Many other ministries also mobilized their resources for this unique moment in history. Relief work, exchange programs and technological and medical assistance were eagerly sought. As they ministered within the Soviet Union, Christian workers reported unprecedented interest in the gospel.

Meanwhile, the longing for freedom in Alex's native land continued to bubble and boil. Many talked about the republics throwing off their communist cloak and seceding from the USSR to form independent states. The world held its breath wondering what would happen next.

Gorbachev continued to reiterate many of the themes he had discussed with the members of Project Christian Bridge group. During an interview with an Italian correspondent, Gorbachev referred to God so often that the correspondent asked, "Mr. Gorbachev, is it true that I hear you using the name of God and of Christ more than we've ever heard it before?"

Gorbachev answered, "There was a group from America who came and visited me a month ago and they made me think seriously about things that I've never thought of before."

Other interviewers also heard his statements and questioned him about his interest in spiritual things. As he had when he met with the American evangelicals, Gorbachev still claimed to be a communist and an atheist, but he also admitted to reading the Bible, saying he was intrigued by the love and forgiveness found within its pages.

How much he admired those concepts was about to be tested. On December 8, Russian President Boris Yeltsin met with the presidents of Belarus and Ukraine. They called for the development of a free market economy and declared the formation of a loose alliance known as the Commonwealth of Independent States (CIS).

The world shook its head, questioning whether the mighty Soviet system would really succumb without bloodshed or roar in fury and once again crush all opposition.

Gorbachev could have ordered military action to preserve his power and the communist regime. Instead, on December 25, 1991, he announced that the Soviet Union was dissolved, thus eliminating an Iron

Curtain empire once thought to be indestructible and surrendering his own position of world leadership.

International reporters attributed the collapse to economic woes, but many Soviet leaders acknowledged that spiritual bankruptcy superseded all other causes. In their analysis, they reflected convictions steadfastly held by generations of godly Russians who lamented their nation's great disasters and untold suffering: "Men have forgotten God; that is why all this has happened."[1]

Sopli's native son, forced to emigrate sixty-two years earlier, had courageously called his compatriots back to God through the long, dark days when God's very existence was denied and denounced. His proclamation of truth had fostered hope and sustained faith, and now, just as Jesus had promised, truth was setting his people free.

I know men; and I tell you that Jesus Christ is no
mere man. Between Him and every other person in
the world there is no possible term of comparison.
Alexander, Caesar, Charlemagne and I have founded
empires. But on what did we rest the creations of our
genius? Upon force. Jesus Christ founded His empire upon love; and at this hour millions of men
would die for Him.

—Napoleon Bonaparte

CHAPTER 18

THESE SAME BRICKS
1992-1993: Moscow; Kobrin,
Belarus; Beltsi, Moldova

CHANGE. LIKE A PENT-UP avalanche, it thundered
through the newly formed CIS. Russia slashed military spending and ended price controls, leading to
soaring prices, bare shelves and long lines for the sim-
plest necessities of life. Destitute, the emerging de-
mocracies looked to the West for humanitarian aid as
they struggled to establish a workable government and
economic system. The people, used to being told what
they could and could not do, scrambled to find their
way in an uncharted labyrinth of liberty.

General Nicolai Stolyarov faced a daunting task as
the Major General of the Russian Military. When

Alex met him in March 1992, Stolyarov said, "Rev. Leonovich, we need at least 3 million Bibles for all those in the military. Since the last time we met, the Soviet Union has been dismantled. Our army has been cut by 170,000 and many who were formerly in the military suddenly find themselves without a home, without a country and without an identity. This is a desperate situation because they do not know where they are going or what the future holds. As a result there has been an epidemic of suicides.

"You've been in the radio ministry for many years. Could you help us get at least 20,000 cassettes on the subject of suicide to tell these people there is hope? If you can't help us, we don't know who can."

Alex wondered where he would get the money to print so many Bibles and produce so many cassettes. Astounded by the enormity of the request but excited by the opportunity, Alex shared the need with American believers, who quickly sent SMS $106,000. Other missions and Bible societies also joined in the effort.

Concerned about those forced out of the military, Stolyarov initiated special institutes to train the officers for civilian work. To assist in the retraining process, he sought American corporations to sponsor short-term, hands-on internships in the United States where he hoped the officers would learn moral principles they could use in implementing a free market system of life, trade and work in the CIS.

When Washington officials heard of Stolyarov's plan, they invited him to speak about it on college and university campuses. Stolyarov immediately called Alex to ask if he would be his interpreter.

"Other people sometimes call that being an interrupter," Alex says jokingly. "Nevertheless, I felt honored to be asked. We were taken by private plane from campus to campus in Iowa, Minnesota, North and South Dakota, Indiana, Illinois and Michigan, speaking as many as five to seven times a day in different areas.

"One afternoon as we were returning from one of the engagements, we stopped at Joel Nederhood's home because I needed to discuss some business relating to his Russian broadcasts. He and I went upstairs while Stolyarov remained downstairs. When Joel and I came down, we saw him reading a New Testament which we had printed years before with special paper so that prisoners who received it could hide it in the ground without its absorbing moisture.

"I didn't know where he got the New Testament, but I walked up and put my arm around his shoulder and said, 'Nikolai Sergeyevitch, *tchto cheetayete?*' ('What are you reading?')

"He showed me where he had just underlined verses in the gospel of John which talk about those who love darkness rather than light because their deeds are evil. Seeing his interest, I explained what it meant.

"From then on, he called me his spiritual father and constantly asked questions about spiritual things as we

231

traveled. One night he said, 'Pavlovich, I made my peace with the Lord.' "

Later that year, General Stolyarov returned to the United States to meet with Senator Mark Hatfield to discuss applying the principles of Christianity to politics. The discussion so impressed Stolyarov that he subsequently wrote a book entitled *Politics Can Be Clean*.

Economic conditions in the CIS continued to force drastic cuts in military spending. Recognizing that the military had been reduced to one-half of its former size, Stolyarov decreased his request for Bibles to one and a half million and his request for cassettes about suicide to 10,000.

Once the Bibles were delivered, Stolyarov made introductory comments in each one, encouraging the recipients to read the Bible at least once in their lifetimes.

◊ ◊ ◊ ◊ ◊ ◊ ◊

In June 1993, Alex traveled to Kobrin to participate in dedication ceremonies for the largest evangelical church in Belarus. Over 4,000 people gathered for the service, including the mayor, the archbishop of the Russian Orthodox Church and local officials who had previously resisted the evangelicals. As they witnessed the dedication service, they said, "We're sorry, but we were forced to oppose you in earlier days."

Alex marveled at the beauty of the building erected so near to his birthplace. With wages averaging only

$12 a month while shoes cost $90, believers were unable to buy supplies. Furthermore, even if they had been able to pay for building materials, few were available.

To remedy the situation, they knocked down old factories and other unused buildings. Then they took the splintered beams and broken bricks to construct a church. Afraid the porous old bricks would absorb moisture and then crack and crumble, they used cement and hard-ground glass to create a type of stucco with which they covered the building.

Looking at the church right after a rain, Alex remarked, "It glistened in the sunshine like India's Taj Mahal."

But the church was more than just a place of rare beauty; it was also an answer to prayers breathed decades earlier. Those building the church found a used World War II shell cemented into the wall of an abandoned missile silo. After carefully chiseling it out of the wall, they found a piece of paper where some Christians had written: "Stalin made us destroy a church building in order to build this missile silo. We are praying that someday these very same bricks may be used to build a church for worshiping God."

When Alex heard the story, he cried, "Hallelujah! We serve a prayer-hearing and a prayer-answering God!"

No one believed that more than Basil, who traveled from Beltsi, Moldova, to rejoice with Kobrin believers and to again ask Alex to take part in the dedication of his church. As Basil crushed Alex with his enthusiastic embrace, he assured Alex that this time his church had received its certificate of occupancy. Then he shouted, "I vowed before God that the house of worship I've built is not going to be dedicated without your presence there."

Basil, persistent as always, would not leave until Alex promised to return for the dedication of the church on October 3.

Later that night, when others in the group had gone to sleep, one of the leaders from the Kobrin church said, "Brother Alex, we know you're tired, but some of us would like to meet with you.

"Just ten kilometers from this church is a military camp that was used to train officers for war. It has 130 acres of fenced land in a radiation-free zone.

"Brother Alex, we can get this place and make a Christian youth camp to use as a rehabilitation center for children who were victims of the Chernobyl accident.

"We could also have a retreat center and eventually a home for the aged, warehouses for Christian literature and perhaps even printing presses to print gospel literature. But we are not able to do it financially. Would you be able to help us?"

Although it was past midnight, Alex suggested that they pray. As they knelt, Alex said, "I don't know where the funds are going to come from or how we're going to do it, but go to it. We'll trust the Lord together."

The next day, Alex met with the mayor, who became very excited about the project. Many other leaders also voiced their support.

When Alex returned to the United States, he spoke of the Kobrin children's camp wherever he went.

In October, he flew to Minsk to deliver $10,000 toward the purchase of the camp before going to Moldova to participate in the dedication of Basil's church. After giving the gift to the leaders of the Kobrin project, Alex boarded a train for Kiev where he was to meet Misha and a man Basil was sending to take them to Beltsi, Moldova.

The driver arrived as scheduled on Friday night, but the group was unable to leave until the next morning. Further delays kept them from leaving until midday. Then, just as they got started, Ukrainian police stopped them because the car had Moldovian plates. Because the countries now had separate governments, the police trumped up charges and insisted that they pay a sizable sum of money before allowing them to go.

Along the way, they had two blowouts, one of which stranded them for four hours until someone could bring a new wheel from Moldova. By the time they finally got to the Moldovian border, it was 2 a.m.

The border guards refused to let Alex and Misha into Moldova without visas. The visitors explained they had been told they could get their visas at the border, but the guards said the office was closed until Monday. Alex and Misha explained their need to be at

Basil's church the next morning. The guards replied, "That's absolutely impossible and there's no way you can do anything about it."

Stymied, Alex and Misha sent the driver back to Moldova to tell the church that they had tried to come and were only two hours away but could not get there because of the problem at the border. Then they asked for a hotel so they could get a few hours of sleep. Alex says: "We were taken to what I would call an excuse for a hotel.

"It cost only 75 cents a night. And, from the outside, it didn't look too bad. But when we walked in, the smell was overwhelming. I don't know when it had last been cleaned. I opened the door to the bathroom and closed it immediately because it was filled with cockroaches, rust, dirt, filth and an unbearable stench.

"By now it was nearly 5 o'clock in the morning and I was exhausted. So, with my clothes on, I lay down on the bed. I put my coat over me to keep a little warmer because there was no heat and it was about thirty degrees.

"I fell asleep, but in what seemed to be five minutes, there was a knock on the door and I saw men in camouflage battle fatigues. I was still a little dazed, but I could see that one of them had red eyes as if he had been drinking all night. 'We hear you need help,' they said.

"I said we did and they said, 'Well, maybe we could help you.'

"I answered, 'But I don't know who you are.' "

Misha, right behind the men, said, "I couldn't sleep at all. I closed my eyes, but suddenly at 6 o'clock, it was as if I heard some kind of a voice saying, *'Spoostees ih ihdjee'* ('Go down and go').

"I didn't know if it was a dream," Misha continued, "but I just felt compelled to do what I felt I'd heard so I went downstairs and saw a *babushka* (an older lady with a kerchief around her head) seated at a desk. She looked up as she heard footsteps and said, 'You can't sleep?' "

"That's right," Misha replied. "We came so far from America to get to Moldova, but we can't get there because of the border guards."

"Maybe I can help you," she said.

Misha thought to himself, *What can that little old lady do?* But before he could speak, she sang out, "But it will cost you money!"

"How much?" Misha asked.

"$10," she replied.

Misha reached into his pocket and gave her the money, having no idea what get-up-and-go lay within the *babushka*. "She went like greased lightning and quickly appeared with these men, one of them a border guard.

Alex rubbed his weary eyes again, wondering if he were still dreaming.

One of the men spoke up: "So you need help? I'll be able to help you just as I have helped others.

Now, the border is on the other side of the river and he" (pointing to the other guard) "is on patrol duty across the river. But it will cost you money. I'll have to get a man to go on the other side of the river to get a car to take you to the city of Beltsi. That will cost you at least $20 and since I'm going to do something that is even more risky, it will cost you $25 more."

Alex and Misha agreed. "Fine, we'll give you the $45. Just see what you can do."

Once they had the money, the men took Alex and Misha to the riverbank. Alex recalls, "The man who was the spokesman told us to stand behind some bushes. He waited until the patrol boat went by and then used binoculars to search the other shore for the taxi which would take us to Beltsi.

"About an hour later, he whispered, 'Hurry, Hurry!' and headed us toward a rowboat with a little four-and-a-half horsepower outboard motor.

"As we got in, I was sure it was going to sink. I didn't have much, but there were three of us and Misha had a big suitcase of supplies.

"When our guide pulled the cord, the motor sputtered weakly and we slowly started going upriver. The boat was barely above the water line and a cold spray kept covering us. Then, suddenly, the anchor slipped into the water, and I got soaked from the splash!

"But that was nothing. When we finally got to the other side, we came ashore at a marshy, muddy area.

238

The guide told us to get out quickly. I tried to step lightly, but the soil gave way under me and I landed on my knee in the mud.

"Then I saw the so-called taxi that was waiting for us. It was not much of an automobile! The driver said, 'This is a risky thing that I'm doing.' . . . And, that, of course, cost us money. We finally negotiated with him to take us where we were going for $70.

"I thought that wasn't too bad a price since it would take him two hours to take us and two hours to come back. But when he started going, first one door flew open and then another, allowing dust to pour in. The driver stopped to tie one door shut with wire, but then the other flew open. Meanwhile, I tried to dry off my muddy knee so I would be somewhat presentable.

"Of course, we had no address for the church since Basil's driver was to have taken us. So we stopped just outside the city to ask about the church. We were told, 'Well, we think there's a church being built, but it's in the other direction from which you are traveling.'

"We went there but were sent to another place where there was to have been a Pentecostal house of prayer. We explained that we were looking for a Baptist house of worship, but the people said they didn't know of any Baptist churches.

"Not knowing what to do, we decided to go to the Pentecostal church to see if they could help us. When we arrived where it was supposed to be, we couldn't see anything that even resembled a house of worship.

Seeing a man carrying a pail of water, we stopped and asked, 'Could you direct us to the Baptist church which is being dedicated today?'

"The man put down the pail of water and looked at us in amazement and asked, 'Are you the brethren from America?'

"When he found out that we were, he said, 'My son-in-law is the man who left at 2 o'clock in the morning to bring you the wheel for the car that had two blowouts. When he came back, he said the border guards weren't letting you through.'

"Then the man ran into his house and left the water pail with his wife, saying, 'I'll tell you all about it later' and jumped into the car with us.

"We would never have found the place without him, and if we had come a second earlier or later, we would not have met him. It was just God's perfect timing.

"When we were just one kilometer from the church, we saw smoke coming through the floorboards and the car stopped. We tried every way to get the car moving, but the gears had jammed and the clutch was burning.

"Finally the driver said, 'You're going to have to push.'

"We got out of the car and started pushing. I forgot that I'd had a heart attack and triple bypass and angioplasty and pushed with the rest.

"All of a sudden, the car took off! I thought, *Dear Lord, what now? All our bags and equipment and supplies are in the car!* But the driver stopped the car, we got back in and he drove in first gear until we got to the church.

"We arrived forty-five minutes after the service had ended, but there were still about 350 people sitting at outside tables set for the occasion. They had held their meeting but not the dedication.

"When Basil saw me he was so excited he couldn't speak. Rushing toward me like a roaring freight train, he embraced me repeatedly, making me glad my head was solidly connected to the rest of my body.

"Then Basil shouted in Russian, 'Didn't I tell you we have a great God? We have a God of miracles! We prayed and we believed that God was going to perform a miracle.'

"Basil threw his hands up while he thanked the great God of heaven for performing a miracle to allow us to be there and the people invited us to eat with them. Then Basil asked everyone to go into the church building for the dedication. There he again told the story of how my message was the last he heard before his arrest and of how he had vowed there would be no dedication unless I could be there.

"Misha and I both presented brief messages and then I invited the elders of the church and the other pastors who were present to raise their hands in dedication of the building to God. The service that had started at 10 o'clock that morning never really ended until 4:30 that afternoon.

"Basil was right: We do serve a great God! Regardless of whether it's a million and a half Bibles for the military, a church built from the bricks of an abandoned missile silo or the harrowing adventures of getting to Basil's dedication ceremonies, God seems to delight in turning circumstances around."

Men reject their prophets and slay them, but they love their martyrs and honour those whom they have slain.

—Feodor Dostoyevsky,
The Brothers Karamazov, Part XV,
Book VI, chapter 3

CHAPTER 19

FROM TRAITOR TO PATRIOT
October 3, 1993; 1994: Moscow

AFTER DEDICATING BASIL'S CHURCH in Beltsi, Alex and Misha boarded a train from Moldova to Kiev. From there, they planned to fly to Moscow. When they got off the train in Kiev on October 3, 1993, however, they learned that Moscow was caught in a crisis as Russian President Boris Yeltsin attempted to end a revolt.

The escalating conflict created havoc, causing many flights to be rerouted or canceled. As Alex and Misha debated whether to put themselves in jeopardy, they received a message from General Stolyarov, now first Assistant Minister in the Department of Defense, saying bodyguards would meet them at the airport to escort them to their hotel. Believing this was God's provision, Alex and Misha decided to risk making the trip.

The flight landed at a different airport than usual. A uniformed guard with an automatic rifle met them and told them that Stolyarov had been brutally attacked because he had refused to participate in the coup against Yeltsin. As the guard escorted them to the Marco Polo Hotel, Alex and Misha heard rumbling tanks and whirring bullets.

Stolyarov's wife, Yelyenna, met them at the hotel and the three of them hired a driver to go to the hospital. She told them her husband had been offered a high position in the new government if he would join the revolt but had replied, "I cannot serve two presidents. I will not be a traitor to one while working under the other."

As he left work that day, a man attacked Stolyarov, spraying mace in his face and beating him with an iron pipe until he collapsed.

Thinking Stolyarov was dead, his assailant took him to the northern outskirts of Moscow and dumped him in a secluded place. Then, to make sure whoever found the general would know he had been attacked because of his unwillingness to join the opposition, the hit man took a pistol which Gorbachev had given Stolyarov in gratitude for his part in breaking the 1991 coup. It was inscribed with the words: "For bravery displayed in the struggle for democracy in Russia."

Several hours passed before Stolyarov regained consciousness. He found himself in a pool of his own blood mixed with grass and leaves. Despite severe injuries and very cold temperatures, he managed to grope his way to a telephone where he called for help and was taken to a military hospital.

Alex and Misha appreciated hearing Yelyenna's account of the attack as they rode to the hospital in a government car without lights via back streets. All around, tracer bullets flew and tanks and machine guns blasted away as Yeltsin's forces attempted to recapture the parliament building.

When the trio arrived at the hospital, they were told that no one, including Yelyenna, was allowed to see Stolyarov.

Prevented from visiting in person, Alex called on the phone. Stolyarov expressed deep appreciation for the call and welcomed Alex's offer to pray with him. He again testified to his own faith by saying, "Alexei Pavlovich, I've made my peace with God."

Later that evening, as the driver dropped Alex and Misha off at their hotel just five blocks from the parliament building, he warned them against venturing out. If they felt compelled to leave the hotel, he added, they should wear dark clothes and be very careful since snipers were firing at anything and light colors would make them more vulnerable.

At the height of the confrontation, coup leaders attempted to take over national broadcast facilities. Hoping to prevent the takeover and civil upheaval, officials countered by playing an archived edition of "The Back to God Hour" on the subject of true peace. Then they suspended operations.

Later that night Yeltsin's troops finally prevailed. His opponents vacated the parliament building carrying a white flag of surrender.

The next day, Alex and Misha walked to the area around the parliament building, now blackened from the artillery assault and still smoking. Sensing the significance of the moment, they picked up some used shells by a barbed wire barricade. A TV camera crew filmed them. That evening the footage of Alex and Misha was televised throughout Russia.

Many people recognized them. Knowing Misha as the voice on "The Back to God Hour," they told him, "We heard your broadcast. Thank you. Thank you."

Yeltsin's decision to use force raised eyebrows in some circles. People wondered if he was truly committed to democracy or was just another dictator depicting himself as democratic.

Alex repeatedly found himself answering that question by saying: "Some have asked whether Yeltsin was wise to move in with power and military force. He had no other choice. That parliament was made up of old-liners who put themselves into power and held back the democratic process of law.

"We need to pray for Mr. Yeltsin. We've laid the groundwork for meeting with him, and if it had not been for this crisis, we would be doing that the early part of December. Our plan is to form a committee of about twenty people on this side and twenty people on that side to have a dialogue so that those from the upper echelon of government can work to resolve things which have been bothering so many people on both sides of the sea.

"Pray that God gives us wisdom. We don't want to go ahead of Him nor do we wish to lag behind. We're seeking the face of God that we may have His wisdom in all the decisions that need to be made."

Misha remained in Russia after Alex returned to the United States. As soon as he learned Stolyarov could have visitors, Misha went to the hospital. He told Alex, "When I visited General Stolyarov, he had two Bibles on the night table next to his bed. One was the English one given to him by Senator Hatfield; the other was the Russian one you gave to him. Both were open to the twenty-third Psalm.

"Stolyarov told me, 'These were difficult moments in my life, and only God's Word helped me to endure this valley of death. Tell Senator Hatfield and Alex Leonovich that the Word of God to which they introduced me shall forever remain in my heart.' "

As Alex and others told of the opening doors in the CIS, Western believers became excited about the escalating opportunities. American and German Christians immediately saw the value of the Chernobyl camp project and donated the $90,000 needed to purchase and renovate the site. German Mennonites arrived with two huge trucks of tractors, equipment and supplies. Young people from Germany and America came with shovels and other tools to clear the grounds and initiate renovations leading to a modern camp facility with more than thirty buildings.

When the city leaders saw what was being accomplished, they said, "If we did not see this with our own eyes, we would not believe that there are such dedicated people."

Alex was besieged with requests and overwhelmed with opportunities. One of the most unusual was an invitation to give a three-week series of lectures on the Bible and humanity at Friendship University, a prestigious school originally built to teach atheism and communism.

Alex recalls: "I was quick to respond and say yes, but after I said yes, I got scared. The only school in the world to grant a degree in scientific atheism had invited me to give a series of lectures on the Bible! How in the period of only three weeks could I prepare to share material that spanned centuries? How could I speak about the Bible without giving them a basic understanding of God? How could I speak about God without talking about the forces of evil and so many other issues?

"Chills ran up and down my body as I thought about it. I felt totally inadequate. I didn't know what else to do but to commit the whole task to the Lord.

"When Babs and I went, we received tremendous attention from everyone. It was a great thrill to look into the faces of the professors and students and declare the living Word of God. While I was in the midst of the lecture series, who should arrive but Basil!

"Basil had heard me talk about the lectures on my 'New Life' radio broadcast. Knowing I'd be in Moscow, he boarded an all-night train and came to search for me. He managed to figure out where we were staying. We, of course, weren't there, so Basil sat in the lobby for over seven hours looking at every face. When he finally saw me, he again bowled me over like a locomotive. Then he opened his portfolio and showed me his certificate: He had just completed Bible school and seminary at the Korean Bible Institute in Moscow to better prepare for his work as a pastor.

"He greeted me by saying, 'I've come like Elisha came to Elijah, Brother Alex, so you can lay your hands on me and so that your blessing might fall on me.'

"I said, 'Dear brother, when I look upon you and how you've served the Lord all these years, I don't feel worthy of wiping the dust off your shoes. And yet you want me to bless you? I need you to bless me.'

"But Basil persisted, 'No, I will not leave until you pray over me and commit me to the Lord. I want God's hand to rest upon me the same way it has rested upon you and God's Spirit to anoint me the same way He has anointed you so that I might be an instrument in the hands of God.'

"I was moved to tears. We went upstairs to my hotel room where we got on our knees. You should have heard Basil weep as I laid my hands on his head and prayed that he might be filled with the power of the Holy Spirit so that God could use him to convey the message of God's redeeming grace and love.

"When I finished, Basil prayed and we embraced. Then he took his portfolio and said, 'Now, brother Alex, I'm going home.' "

Alex thought of Basil many times as he lectured to the university students. At the end of the series, Friendship University officials held a banquet in Alex's honor where they awarded him an honorary doctorate in the fields of religion and philosophy, the first honorary doctorate ever given to a foreigner. Always too busy ministering to others to earn advanced degrees, Alex felt a great sense of gratitude and humility as he accepted the degree.

To commemorate the occasion, Alex was given a medallion inscribed: "In honor of your major influence in the spiritual and humanitarian uniting of the country of Russia."

Time and truth had finally triumphed over the trumped-up charges of being a traitor!

When God measures a man, He puts the tape around the heart instead of the head.

—Anonymous

CHAPTER 20

ALL HEART
1995 - Present

SAILOR BOY, GOSPEL KID, greenhorn, prankster, musician, preacher, evangelist, radio broadcaster, missionary, "traitor," pastor, administrator, translator, networker, humanitarian, patriot . . . so many different identities. Yet even if Alex were to wear all of his titles at one time, they would not tell the real story of who he is or why his ministry has been so effective.

"Alex is genuine," Dr. George Boltniew, pastor and field representative for SMS, states. "His voice is recognized by many thousands in North and South America and by millions in Europe. His programs are some of the best ever produced in Russian, but the real essence of his ministry is his willingness to serve. He never refuses anyone anything."

"Alex is a man with a woman's heart," his mother once said. "He can laugh hard with you, but he can also cry hard. He's a man's man, but he's also very sensitive and very caring like a woman. He has traits of both, just like God."

Babs says, "Everyone says my husband has a heart problem: He's all heart."

Ironically, most of Alex's health problems have been heart-related: A genetic predisposition to over-producing unhealthy cholesterol has resulted in a major heart attack, two angioplasties and triple coronary artery bypass surgery.

Although heart disease has slowed Alex down, it has never really stopped him. Instead, the difficulties of life simply change Alex's place of ministry. When he can travel, the world is his mission field. When his physical heart demands rest, the hospital is his parish. Wherever he is or whatever his state of well-being, Alex shares the love of Christ.

In 1995, Alex celebrated fifty years of full-time ministry with continuous radio outreach to the people of Russia. In his role as president of RUEBU, he was invited to return to Buenos Aires, Argentina, to serve as a member of the General Council of Baptist World Alliance. While there, he was honored for his fifty years of uninterrupted ministry among the Slavic peoples of the world. Those touched by his ministry in South America were especially excited by his return to the continent where he began his gospel broadcasts.

God's call has taken Alex to every inhabited continent. Regardless of where he goes, Alex stands tall in proclaiming truth while bending low to show love. Whether preaching God's Word or passing out pieces of gum to children, he exudes the love of God to young and old, rich and poor, famous and unknown.

Giving to others, however, never outranks his wholehearted devotion to his wife and family. Babs frequently says, "He's a wonderful man and I don't really deserve him."

She says this remembering her vow to never marry a "greenhorn" and her stilted reaction when Alex came home from South America unexpectedly. With a twinkle in her eyes, she says, "Alex sometimes asks if I'm ready to tell him what's wrong yet. I just smile and say, 'I love you now more than ever.' "

Alex, of course, sees a different side of the situation. He cannot praise Babs enough. "She's a marvelous companion and helpmeet, always cheerfully and joyfully serving together with me. Our children love her and our grandchildren swarm around her. She's not pushy or forward, preferring to stay in the background, but she's a great supporter and solidifying force. That's a great help because if you have two heads, you have a monster."

Alex's ability to balance good humor with seriousness of purpose enables him to be resilient through ever-changing challenges. Recognizing that God is the One who calls people to Himself in a wide variety of ways and through many different people, Alex has not even attempted to compile statistics. Russian pastors, however, have often reported that eighty to ninety percent of those seeking believer's baptism during the height of the communist regime said they were introduced to Christianity through shortwave radio programs.

As the longest-running Russian gospel broadcast, "New Life" has played—and continues to play—a primary role in bringing people to Christ. Alex's faithful proclamation of truth regardless of political regime required great courage and stamina. His integrity and genuine concern for the Russian people built trust and relationships that nudged open numerous doors of opportunity for SMS and many other ministries.

Yet, like the rest of the world, Alex felt he was caught off guard when the Iron Curtain crumbled and opportunities for the gospel exploded. Astounded by the implosion of Soviet communism, news commentators quickly attributed it to economic woes and political bureaucracy even though Gorbachev and other high-ranking Soviet officials often referred to an underlying spiritual and moral crisis.

NRB President E. Brandt Gustavson notes that "Some feel that Christian broadcasting was a significant factor in the demise of communism because it kept belief in God alive."

And what a belief in God it was! Individuals and families huddled under blankets while straining to hear God's Word via short-wave radio signals jammed by the government. Christians boldly attending church services even though they knew they would be excluded from higher education or job promotions.

Men like Basil, who risked persecution, imprisonment and martyrdom to share the Word of God.

Multitudes of Russian believers prayed fervently and kept the faith, even under great persecution. Their greatest desire was to remain faithful to God in the place where He had put them. Alex believes their faith under pressure is a louder sermon than anything he or anyone else preaches.

The need to pray for Slavic Christians has not evaporated because communism no longer reigns. While grateful for their new freedoms, Russian believers also recognize the potential problems which accompany liberty and ask for prayer to remain faithful to God even while enjoying greater freedom.

Freedom, of course, is not guaranteed. Russian laws concerning religious freedom continue to vacillate. The open policy instituted in the 1980s allowed many different denominations and cults to enter the fifteen nations once known as the Soviet Union. Some groups understood Slavic thinking and respected Slavic heritage; others imported their own ideas and exploited the people. Currently, new laws and regulations are being drafted and implemented, leaving evangelicals wondering about their future.

Some fear the new laws will greatly curtail evangelistic efforts, especially the work of foreign missionary organizations. While wisdom mandates vigilance, Alex refuses to let fear paralyze his ministry: "SMS is not an outside organization; we do everything within the local evangelical movement there. We are they; they are we. And because the parliament originally enacting the laws no longer exists, some of the laws may be changed."

At a time of life usually considered retirement years, Alex repeatedly states he is busier than ever: "To me, retirement is a foreign word. I'm going stronger and faster than ever before and living on wings and wheels."

In addition to over forty years of involvement with SMS, Alex has also served two four-year terms as the president of RUEBU, the oldest outreach to Slavic people in North America. Since *glasnost* and *perestroika* were first introduced in 1985, over 3 million Slavs have emigrated to the United States, creating a burgeoning mission field stateside. More than fifty new congregations have sprung up in Florida, North Carolina, West Virginia, New England, the Midwest and on the West Coast. Both the children's camps and adult conferences at Ashford, Connecticut saw record crowds in 1998.

While Alex fulfills his responsibilities with the diligence which has characterized his life, he also recognizes the need to turn the reins over to a new generation. He has vested the SMS board with a mandate to find a successor. His thought is not of retirement but of extending his service for the Lord by equipping others to continue the work of reaching his people with the gospel.

The Russian people have long been known as God-seekers. Centuries of injustice, bondage and persecution have repeatedly crushed, but never extinguished, that pursuit.

Author Alexander Solzhenitsyn has devoted himself to studying the history of the Russian revolution. After reading hundreds of books, interviewing hundreds of people and writing many books of his own, Solzhenitsyn made this statement when receiving the 1983 Templeton Award: "If I were asked today to formulate as concisely as possible the main cause of the ruinous revolution that swallowed up some 60 million of our people, I could not put it more accurately than to repeat: 'Men have forgotten God; that's why all this has happened.'

"I myself see Christianity today as the only living spiritual force capable of undertaking the spiritual healing of Russia."[1]

Alex has invested his life in helping meet that need by consistently speaking to the Russian soul. He says, "As I look back over the years, it's been a difficult road. How many times we've experienced difficulties: financial, physical and attacks of the adversary! Discouragements have come, but isn't it wonderful how God sends us blessings to recharge our batteries and keep us going?

"Today, I am grateful to God that He coaxed me to follow him. If someone were to ask me, 'Did you make a mistake in doing what you did?' I can honestly say that if I had life to live over again, I wouldn't change anything.

"Today I rejoice as I remember the problems of yesteryear because they became blessings in disguise. The difficulties of life brought me closer to God and taught me the value of things that too many take for granted. I think of the little things that seem so insignificant to others, but to me they're very meaningful. I've learned to depend on what God can do rather than on what I'm able to do.

"I'm overwhelmed with the way God works and weaves things together. To be able to go and minister to others is a privilege. The Lord has no other hands, no other feet, no other lips than the lips, the feet, the hands of His own people. The great thrill is to be an instrument in the hands of the Master Worker, allowing His Spirit to work first in our own hearts and then to work through us to accomplish what we in our own strength can never do.

"If I were to pick one word to describe my life, it would be 'Fulfilled!' "

With a heart for the soul of Russia, Alex Leonovich has loved and served both his God and his people.

His motto, "No sacrifice too great; no job too big; no place too far; whatever, whenever, wherever," has given Alex the fulfillment that Jesus promised when He said:

> Whoever desires to come after Me, let
> him deny himself, and take up his cross,
> and follow Me. For whoever desires to
> save his life will lose it, but whoever loses
> his life for My sake and the gospel's will

save it. For what will it profit a man if he gains the whole world, and loses his own soul? Or what will a man give in exchange for his soul? (Mark 8:34-37, NKJV)

ENDNOTES

Chapter 9 - Heart for Home
1 Dr. Paul E. Freed, quoted by David Fisher, Trans World Radio
2 Michael Rowe, *Russian Revolution* (London: HarperCollins, 1994), p. 163.

Chapter 11 - A Growing Hunger
1 Rowe, p. 163.
2 Paul E. Freed, *Towers to Eternity* (Chatham, NJ: Trans World Radio, 1994), pp. 187-188.

Chapter 12 - "Did You Bring Bread?"
1 *The Link* (South River, NJ: SMS, July, 1981), p. 6.

Chapter 15 - Revolution or Reformation?
1 Philip Yancey, *Praying with the KGB* (Portland, OR: Multnomah, 1992), p. 24.
2 Ibid., p. 25.
3 Ibid., p. 27.

Chapter 16 - Forgiving the KGB
1 Ibid., p. 43.
2 Ibid., p. 44.
3 Ibid., p. 45.
4 Ibid., p. 46.
5 Ibid., p. 47.
6 Ibid.

Chapter 17 - Back to Sopli
1 Ibid., p. 89.

Chapter 20 - All Heart
1 Ibid.

Acronyms:

AUCECB: All-Union Council of Evangelical Christians-Baptists. Sometimes referred to as the Evangelical Baptist Union. Renamed Union of Evangelical Christians-Baptists (UECB) in 1990.

CIS: Commonwealth of Independent States

CPR: Council of Prisoners' Relatives

DPs: Displaced Persons

EPA: Evangelical Press Association

FEBC: Far East Broadcasting Company

HCJB: Heralding Christ Jesus' Blessings. Now HCJB World Radio.

KGB: Soviet secret police

NRB: National Religious Broadcasters

RBC: Radio Bible Class. Now RBC Ministries.

RGA: Russian Gospel Association. Became Slavic Gospel Association (SGA) in 1949.

RMS: Russian Missionary Service. When Alex became the Executive Secretary in 1958, he requested that the name be changed to Slavic Missionary Service to reflect its outreach to all those of Slavic heritage.

SGA: Slavic Gospel Association

SMS: Slavic Missionary Service

RUEBU: Russian-Ukrainian Evangelical Baptist Union

TWR: Trans World Radio

UECB: Union of Evangelical Christians-Baptists

USSR: Union of Soviet Socialist Republics or Soviet Union

YFC: Youth For Christ